Building the
Sky Bunny

Building the
Sky Bunny

Bill Warner

TAB BOOKS

Blue Ridge Summit, PA

FIRST EDITION
FIRST PRINTING

© 1992 by **TAB Books**.
TAB Books is a division of McGraw-Hill, Inc.

Based on articles from *Model Builder Magazine*.

Library of Congress Cataloging-in-Publication Data

Warner, Bill.
    Building the sky bunny / by Bill Warner.
      p.   cm.
    Includes index.
    ISBN 0-8306-2531-3 (p.)
    1. Airplanes—Models—Design and construction. I. Title.
  II. Title: Building the sky bunny.
TL770.W284   1991
629.133'134—dc20   91-24237
                                 CIP

Acquisitions Editor: Jeff Worsinger
Book Editor: April D. Nolan
Production: Katherine G. Brown
Book Design: Jaclyn J. Boone

Contents

Acknowledgments   vii

About the Author   xi

Introduction   xiii

1 Getting Ready to Build   1
   Making your own plans   3
   Making your own printwood   4
   Cutting out the parts   4
   Separating the parts   6
   Studying the "road map"   7
   Examining the Sky Bunny plan   7

2 Construction Techniques   11
   Three ways to line up the spar notches   11
   Building the tail   16
   The wing and the pylon slider assembly   16
   The nose   16
   Finishing the wings and tail frames   17
   A bit more on dihedral   21

3 Finishing and Flying   25
   Bending the landing gear   25
   Bending the propeller shaft   30

Covering *31*
Dope *34*
Cleaning up *37*
Pre-flight check *37*
At the field *38*
Trim tabs *39*

Appendix   Suppliers and Publications   49

Glossary   53

Index   57

Acknowledgments

I would like to accord special thanks to Mr. Bill Northrop and *Model Builder Magazine* for commissioning the ''Hey Kid!'' series that was the basis for this book. His encouragement and permission to reprint the material has made this book a reality.

Thanks are also due Sandy Peck and her late husband, Bob, for their valuable support in making available through Peck Polymers all of the materials and kits necessary for the beginning modeler working with this series, and for giving their kind permission to reproduce plans from their kits in this book.

To Jim Kaman, without whose great artwork the series would have been diminished immensely, I add a personal ''well done!''

To the memory of Walt Mooney
1926 – 1990

About the Author

*T*he trouble with many books for beginners in any area is that they are often written by experts in the field who have little experience working with young people or vice-versa.

Bill Warner, a modeler for 50 years and winner of many national model contests, is also a career teacher. In addition to teaching modeling and basic aeronautics in the Los Angeles Public Schools, he also taught classes in aeromodeling at the Summer Science Workshop of the California Museum of Science and Industry over a 17-year period. In his spare time, Bill wrote for model magazines, had model designs published, and sponsored model clubs such as the Sepulveda Balsa Butchers and the Revere Model Aircraft Society.

His most recent efforts include the 14-part series on which this book is based which was published in *Model Builder Magazine* from November 1987 to December 1988. He is a past president and newsletter editor of the Los Angeles-based Flightmasters club, is the Scale Editor of the *National Free Flight Society Digest*, and the Free-Flight Scale columnist for *Model Aviation* magazine, the official publication of the Academy of Model Aeronautics for the past 13 years.

Introduction

*T*his is the second book in a series of three to help beginning aeromodelers. The material originally appeared as a 14-part series in *Model Builder Magazine* and was entitled "Hey Kid! Ya Wanna Build a Model Airplane?" The magazine received so many requests for reprints that it was decided to do it up in book form with as few changes as possible. The material in this book was originally covered in chapters 6–10 of the magazine series and might be considered as an intermediate stage. For the benefit of readers just joining without benefit of having worked through the basic material in the first book, a few important points are reviewed herein.

Although the series is a basic course in building flying models, it has also proven valuable for a large number of older modelers who dropped out for many years and are now getting interested again.

Having worked closely with beginners since 1960, I have seen most of the mistakes that can be made, and I have designed an approach that will help smooth the way, as well as give the reasons for why things are done the way they are. This is a book in basic aeronautics as well as a how-to guide.

In book one, *A Beginning Guide to Building the Peck R.O.G*, modifications to popular ready-made models, the Sleek Streeks, helped the beginning modeler with the basics of model construction and flight. The Peck R.O.G. was an introduction to stick-and-tissue modeling. Book 3, *The Flying Aces Moth*, will cover advanced techniques.

The projects covered in the series were chosen because of their easy availability by mail from one supplier. Other models are available, and the techniques covered can be applied to any model. The models were also chosen for their flyability, and for illustrating specific techniques.

Combining photos with superb line drawings by artist and master modeler Jim Kaman makes some of the toughest going seem easy. It is the next best thing to having your own personal tutor!

This book was written by a career teacher and life-long aeromodeler who has started several hundreds of young people on their way to the skies. It should prove invaluable to Scout leaders and other adults who work with youth groups as well as to individual modelers, young and old.

Included here are many photos of the project in its various stages, as well as superb line illustrations, which serve as visual enhancements to the instructions. And you, the model builder, have a choice: to build from a kit or to create the pieces from unmarked balsa. Either way, the plans are provided (as are complete instructions about how to enlarge them to full-size, and even print them right onto your wood) to make this a thorough and useful book.

A complete list of model supply sources is also included to help you find and order the necessary tools and materials.

Author Bill Warner holding his Free-Flight Stinson SR-7 Reliant, with which he won first place at the U.S. Free-Flight Championships in Taft, California, in 1987.

Chapter **1**

Getting ready to build

*T*he Sky Bunny is an intermediate model I designed especially for this book (available as a kit from Peck Polymers) with some specific ideas in mind having to do with skills development. It will be a good lead-in to your first model with a "built-up" fuselage—the Flying Aces Moth.

All skills will help you with building any model, except perhaps those made of styrofoam, and that is another hobby altogether . . .

To start with, I am going to give you two choices, to build the kit, or to try *scratch-building*. For a scratch-built model, you buy all the parts separately and make up the kit yourself. This is a lot cheaper than buying a kit model, but is a lot of trouble if you don't intend to keep building models with the left-over supply of materials you are going to have. Many modelers prefer to build from plans instead of kits so they can personally pick their own wood at a hobby shop. One kit manufacturer (not Peck), has a reputation for selecting wood so heavy that it seems to have come from the Petrified Forest . . . talk about making non-flying models!

If you want to try scratch building, here's what you'll need for the Sky Bunny:

- 1 sheet medium balsa $1/16$ inch $\times$ 3 inches $\times$ $11^3/4$ inches
- 14 balsa sticks (medium), $3/32$ inch square (get 2 ten-packs from Peck)
- 1 hard balsa stick for fuselage $3/16$ inch $\times$ $3/8$ inch $\times$ 24 inches (or two $11^3/4$-inch lengths from Peck and splice. They don't ship long pieces)
- 1 pc. aluminum tubing $1/16$-inch inside diameter ($3/32$-inch outside)
- 1 large glass bead, or two or three $1/8$-inch brass washer with .050-inch hole (Peck's PA-31)

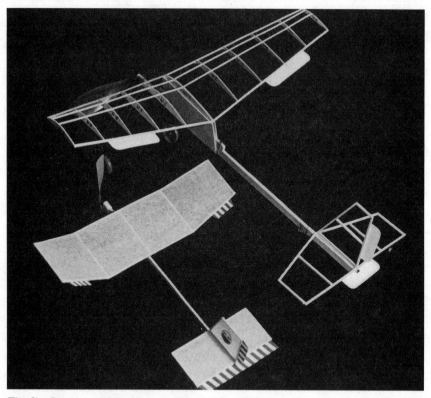

The Sky Bunny (right) was designed to take the builder a step beyond the Peck R.O.G. (left). It teaches advanced built-up wing construction and allows the wing to be moved for aerodynamic balance.

- 1 piece music wire, .046 inch (or .031 inch, which bends easier for kids or arthritis victims), 11¾ inches long for landing gear
- 1 pair 1-inch-diameter wheels
- 1 sheet tissue paper ("domestic" is cheaper, "Japanese" is better)
- 1 plastic propeller, 8-inch (PA-23) or 7-inch (PA-22). (I used the 8-inch one)
- 1 piece .031-inch music wire for prop shaft, 4 inches long. You can substitute ready-made prop shaft from Peck's 10-pack (PA-44)
- 1 small bottle of SIG "Lite-Coat" or similar nonshrinking (called nontautening) clear model dope. Colored dope is not recommended
- 1 bottle or can of thinner for above dope, same size or larger as the dope bottle, as you are going to mix it 50/50 with dope (plus a little for brush cleaning)
- 1 tube Testor's "Cement for Wood Models, Fast Drying, No. 3505" in the green tube (or similar cellulose acetate cement for WOOD models—not plastic cement)

- 1 pkg. 5-minute epoxy for nose-bearing tube (OPTIONAL—stronger than Green Tube, but not essential)
- 1 spool thread
- 1 pkg. dressmaker's straight pins
- 1 modeling knife (X-Acto 8B with flat orange handle is my favorite) or single-edge razor blade(s)
- 1 building board
- 1 roll clear plastic kitchen wrap.

MAKING YOUR OWN PLANS

One of the neatest things ever is the photocopy or Xerox machine which can copy, enlarge, or reduce things you put on it! If you have a smaller propeller than the one a plan indicates, you can have your plan reduced until it is just the right match and then build it that way. If you want to make a Sky Bunny with a gas engine, you can have it blown up until it is about 30-inch span and mount an .020 engine on it. The machine does not have to be able to produce an entire one-piece plan, as you can do it in sections and glue 'em together. You can, for example, enlarge the small plan of the Sky Bunny to 18 inches (standard size) from the one in this book.

Check your telephone book for copy or printing shops if you can't find a machine that will work at school or work. If you live way out in the country, you might even have to mail it someplace, or even draw it up to the size you want, multiplying all the dimensions by 1.3—or whatever size you want—with your pocket calculator.

Modern photocopy machines can copy plans out of a book and enlarge them at the same time.

MAKING YOUR OWN PRINTWOOD

When you buy a model kit, it generally has either die-cut wood or printwood in it. Die-cut kits have parts that have already been punched out for you, and printwood kits have the parts printed on balsa sheet for you to cut out yourself. Good modelers prefer printwood because they can cut their parts out a little oversize and cut or sand them for an exact fit. Some die-cutting ruins the parts, so manufacturers sometimes use harder wood for this process—not good for a light model!

If you want to make your own printwood, there are three different methods you can use to transfer the plans to the wood. If you want to save your original plan, however, you'll need to make a photocopy first and work from that. Making a copy also allows for enlargement or reduction as necessary. Always check the machine you are using to be certain the size of reduction/enlargement is consistent. Some machines have the habit of automatically switching back to full size, and it's important that your proportions are the same. Also, be sure to get an extra copy of any part outlines that will need to be cut from balsa sheet.

Have the machine set to print as dark as you can without smudging the white spaces between the lines. There are all kinds of photocopying machines, and they print quite differently sometimes. The carbon deposited on the sheet can usually be transferred to balsa wood by using a hot iron directly on the back of the copy.

Tape the copy face down on your wood sheet, making sure the grain of the wood runs from the LE to the TE for ribs, and try ironing on the back of the paper. Peek under one end and see if the lines are transferring to your sheet. Experimenting with scrap is always a good idea.

If the hot-iron trick doesn't work, next try a little thinner or acetone on a bit of cotton or rag. Apply this to the copy—not too sloppy or the lines will smudge! Peek under an end to see how it is coming along, and don't be too proud to test the technique on scrap balsa to get the feel of it.

A third method is to cement the paper onto the balsa with rubber cement or a lightly sprayed coat of spray cement for paper and cut the parts out right through the paper. The paper can then be peeled off (encouraged by thinner or lighter fluid if it has dried too long). Some modelers prefer to just poke little holes through the part outline on the plan right into the wood and then play ''connect the dots'' with a ball-point pen. If you use a pen, get all the ink sanded off, or it might bleed through your tissue covering job later on. You could also use carbon paper, there being no limits to a good modeler's imagination. Whichever method you use, just make sure the plan is taped down to the wood so it can't move while you are transferring the shapes!

CUTTING OUT THE PARTS

When you cut out your parts, you always have to decide where on the line to cut. Lines are always wider than the knife cut. If you feel lucky, cut right down the middle. If you are the more cautious type, cut along the *outside* edge of the line and sand it to size later with your sanding block.

① PLAN → BALSA

IRON-ON

FOR BOTH THESE METHODS PLACE COPY UPSIDE DOWN ON WOOD

② COTTON BALL MOISTENED WITH DOPE THINNER OR ACETONE

SOLVENT TRANSFER

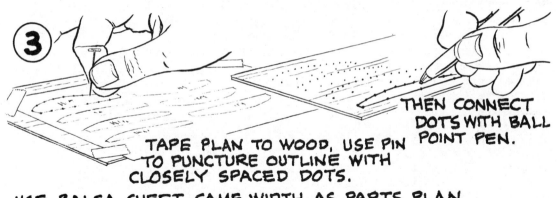

③ TAPE PLAN TO WOOD, USE PIN TO PUNCTURE OUTLINE WITH CLOSELY SPACED DOTS.

THEN CONNECT DOTS WITH BALL POINT PEN.

USE BALSA SHEET SAME WIDTH AS PARTS PLAN

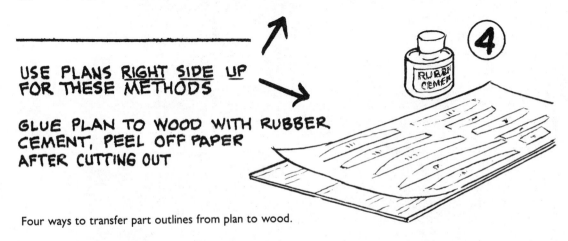

USE PLANS RIGHT SIDE UP FOR THESE METHODS

④ GLUE PLAN TO WOOD WITH RUBBER CEMENT, PEEL OFF PAPER AFTER CUTTING OUT

RUBBER CEMENT

Four ways to transfer part outlines from plan to wood.

If you are making the model from a kit, be sure to sand off any printing that might show through the tissue after covering. Smooth the tops of the ribs (the parts that form the cambered shape of the wing), and round the top edges slightly where the tissue will touch them.

I suggest cutting each rib a little longer than it is shown and trimming it exactly to fit where it goes. It is easier to take it off than to put it back on, and finding one short rib is always a disappointment.

Cutting board

I know that you aren't going to cut on your mom's table, but I'd like to remind you to use something other than another table, plan, or building board. A bit of solid cardboard, linoleum tile, or an old phone book (rip off the cut pages) will work fine and save your plan. Building boards contain grit that dulls knives.

Sharpening your model knife

Sometimes model knives need resharpening. When they start tearing wood, it's time to sharpen them. Ideally, you should use a medium and then a fine whetstone with oil, drawing the blade away from the cutting edge. Hold the blade at just a little more than the original edge so the very edge will contact the stone. The blade can be finished by stropping back and forth on a piece of leather belt glued to the edge of a piece of wood. A little jewelers' rouge on it will make it even more effective. Still, you might prefer just to replace the blade when it gets dull.

SEPARATING THE PARTS

Once you have all the parts laid out on the balsa sheet, take your knife and cut between them, staying away from the part outlines. This will make each one easier to handle. Then, trim away the scrap down to the line. Make several light cuts when cutting *across* the grain to avoid splitting. If you can't tell which way the grain runs from the grain lines on the wood surface, you'll find out soon enough when you try to cut it. When you cut with the grain (same direction as the lines) it cuts like hot butter. Across the grain, it breaks easily.

Grain direction

Balsa's strength runs with the grain. You can tell this by noting how much pressure it takes to break balsa scrap with the grain. The reason we run the grain from end to end on wing ribs is because they need to have strength the long way, from LE to TE. If the grain ran vertically on them, they would buckle easily. On the pylon of the Sky Bunny, the grain needs to go from the fuselage to the wing (vertically). If the grain went longways of the pylon, horizontally, the wing could break off easily. To get the grain in the right direction, the pylon is not laid out in one piece, which would have fit nicely on the balsa sheet, but in two parts, which is harder, but keeps the grain going in the right direction. The drawing of the Bunny on the side is to help you get them together in the right order!

STUDYING THE "ROAD MAP"

Just as a road map of Massachusetts is probably not going to show Henry's Bar and Grill in downtown Framingham, a model plan might leave some of your questions unanswered, and you will need to apply some common sense and try to guess what would make the most sense. The main stuff will be on the plan. Many plans give you step-by-step instructions telling you how to proceed, just as the auto club can give you directions to get to Henry's. I know there is always a temptation to ignore the directions, but a few minutes studying them can save you a lot of problems later on.

The guy who drew the plan and built the model probably had everything drawn to fit right, but often the plan is printed on one machine and the printwood is printed on another. Machines sometimes enlarge or reduce slightly. It is not a bad idea to measure the place where a rib will fit on the plan, and then measure a rib on the printwood. If you find a problem, you can either leave the parts a bit oversize to compensate by making the plane a bit smaller. If you are photocopying plans, always double check with a ruler.

EXAMINING THE SKY BUNNY PLAN

Always try to figure out what the designer had in mind. Look at the nose of the fuselage. Can you figure out that the thread is wound on for strength after the front end is glued together? Notice that the winds of thread are spaced apart a little, to let the glue get around them. I have seen many kids wind it on solidly, like on a spool, figuring that it will be stronger that way—but glue can't penetrate through these thread layers and the front end will be weaker because of it! Assume the designer did it the way it is shown for a reason, unless you have reason to believe he/she was dropped on his/her head as a baby.

If you decide to order just the materials instead of the kit from Peck Polymers, you'll have to order two lengths of fuselage wood because that's the size they ship. You can then splice them together, using an angle cut at the joint to give you more gluing surface. Another thing you might notice on the plan is that I took pains to tell you not to glue the pylon slider assembly to the fuselage. It is movable for flight adjustment, and also lets you take it apart. Ignore the note on the plan at your own risk! Some of you might have already glued it on. That's how we learn . . .!

Dihedral

Continuing your study of the plan, you will notice that the rib named "W-1" ("W" for *wing* and "1" for *first*) is the *root rib*. This is where the wing attaches to the fuselage (or pylon, in this case). It does not stand up straight from the plan at 90 degrees. The top end of the root rib leans slightly toward the wing tip. Why? Because the wing will be assembled later with *vee* dihedral (wing tips higher than the roots) for stability. Some builders might even leave the root ribs out until the dihedral angle is glued in and then put the root ribs in, splitting the difference in their lean between the two wings at that time.

However, I have included a *dihedral gauge*, which can be glued on a bit of scrap balsa or card stock and which can be used to lean the root rib just the right amount. Model plans usually include a dihedral sketch to give you a dimension for the amount of rise at the wing tip. Study this sketch carefully. Sometimes it is measured at the tip of one wing with the other lying flat on the table. If the other wing is up in the air, and the dimension is from the horizontal as if the plane was flying, the dimension given will be only half of what it would be measured the first way. If you put 4 inches of prop under one wing tip of the Sky Bunny, that will be 2 inches under each tip, right? If you put 4 inches under *each* tip, your model will look like it is involved in a hold-up and will be losing a lot of lift! The dihedral is necessary for *lateral*, or side-to-side, stability and will help your model level its wings automatically in turns and gusts.

The prop shaft and thrust line

Notice that there are two styles of propeller shaft shown. Both work. You might try bending one of each to see which is easier for you. Look closely at the nose drawing. You will see that the aluminum tube bearing that the prop shaft fits in is pointed a bit *down* and *right* (as seen from the top). This is important; if you build it in, your model will fly correctly. The *down* keeps the line of the model's thrust coming from the propeller pulling the nose down a bit, thereby holding the angle of attack of the wing down so it will not get too much lift under the power burst.

When the model is going fast with a tightly-wound rubber motor, it is already getting lots of lift from the extra airspeed going over the wing, and killing a little of that with down thrust will keep you from stalling or looping. As the rubber wind down, it will let the model slow, and the down thrust will become less and less effective until it becomes of no importance in the unpowered glide phase of the flight. If you had added weight to the nose to hold it down under power, it would still be there when the power ran out. Your model would then be nose-heavy, and it would dive on the glide. The side thrust helps compensate for the *torque reaction*, or tendency of the model to go left when the prop is spinning right. Remember, the thrust angles for the model were arrived at with the sizes of tubing and shaft shown. A bigger shaft will take up more space in the tube and give you more angle, while a smaller wire will be pulled into less angle due to the sloppier fit.

The Peck kit will have both an aluminum tube and a nylon nose bearing, allowing you to decide on which you would like to use. They could have included a ready-made landing gear and nose assembly, but you are doing this to learn techniques, so I advised against it.

Just as no sane driver would try to drive in a strange city without looking at a road map, you should not try to build a strange model without first studying the plans and instructions. If you have studied the plan and still don't understand something, ask someone else to take a look at it. If that fails, try what the British call "muddling through." It is better to go ahead and do your best rather rather than to give up. Often when you get building it, it will become clear. Sometimes you might have to do something over to get it right, but if you give up, you will never have a finished model.

Chapter 2

Construction Techniques

*T*ime to build! Flatten your plan on the building board, tape it down, and tape a sheet of plastic wrap over it to prevent sticking. Make sure all the wrinkles are out.

Before you start, make a notching tool for those little cutout places in the ribs where the spar sticks are going to go on top of the wings. When you cut them out with a knife, they sometimes split or vary in size. This way you can sand them in.

Take a piece of very hard balsa or other hard wood the width of the spar sticks (3/32 inch). Glue the edge onto a piece of 100-grit garnet paper or something similar. It doesn't take much longer to make six than it does to make one, so why not make some extras? When the glue is dry, trim off the sandpaper even with the sides of the notching stick with an old, single-edged razor blade, such as you buy in paint stores. (Don't ruin your model knife on it!) Then sand the edges to bring them down even with the width of the notcher, using your sanding block. You then will be able to use the notching tool to sand just-right notches into the ribs for the wing spars. You can even glue a strip of balsa along the side to act as a depth stop if all the notches are going to be the same.

THREE WAYS TO LINE UP THE SPAR NOTCHES

Probably the best way to get the spar notches right is to pin the LE down to the plan (× the pins over the wood; don't stick them through it!), and glue the ribs to the LE, *not* to the plan. I suggest *double-gluing*, that is, letting a light coat of glue soak in before adding the second and final assembly coat and joining the parts. I use one or two pins shoved at an angle through the sides of the ribs at an angle to hold them down to the board.

Here the Sky Bunny flies nice and slow on a low-power test for the camera. Good proportions plus adjustment tabs make it a good trainer.

Now, sight straight down over the TE end of each rib, and see if it is lined up with the inside edge of the TE line on the plan. Trim it to size with a razor blade right on the board. If you left the ribs a little long when you cut them out, you are in good shape when it comes to trimming them to exact size now.

Using the dihedral gauge, lean W-1 rib (root rib) inward to match the angle on the gauge. Check this rib in a few minutes to make sure it hasn't moved. Now glue on the TE to all the ribs, using straight pins at each rib location to push in. Work on another part of the model while all this is drying. I use Testors Green Tube glue for all the wood work, but white glue or aliphatic resin glues will work, too. Wipe off excess glue with a piece of scrap stick so you won't have to try to remove it later when it is hard. Making a little glue *fillet* (a drop with most of the extra scraped off) where the parts join is not a bad idea for extra strength, just don't leave gobs of useless glue on the model.

Instant glue is **not recommended** for safety reasons. Your eyes are precious. If you ignore my advice on this one, at least wear safety glasses.

When the glue is dry, line up a straightedge or ruler over the rib

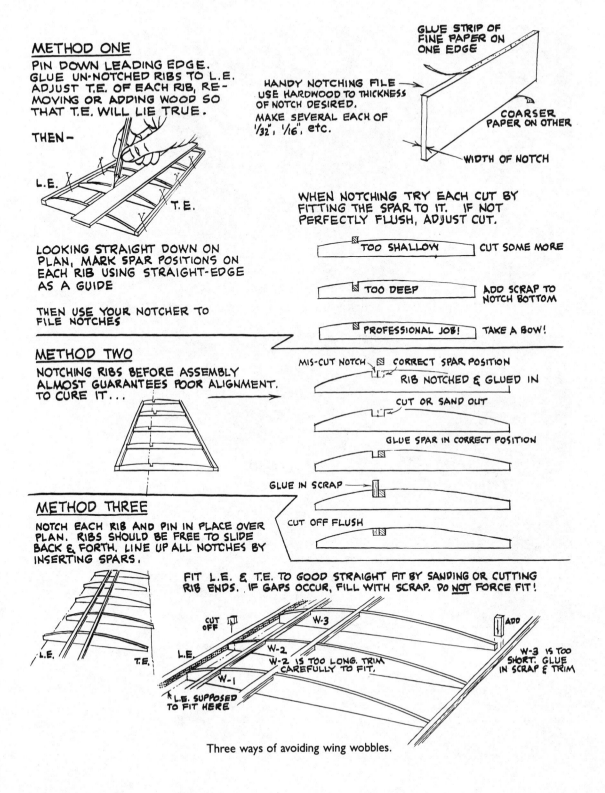

METHOD ONE

PIN DOWN LEADING EDGE.
GLUE UN-NOTCHED RIBS TO L.E.
ADJUST T.E. OF EACH RIB, RE-
MOVING OR ADDING WOOD SO
THAT T.E. WILL LIE TRUE.

THEN—

L.E.

T.E.

LOOKING STRAIGHT DOWN ON
PLAN, MARK SPAR POSITIONS ON
EACH RIB USING STRAIGHT-EDGE
AS A GUIDE

THEN USE YOUR NOTCHER TO
FILE NOTCHES

GLUE STRIP OF
FINE PAPER ON
ONE EDGE

HANDY NOTCHING FILE →
USE HARDWOOD TO THICKNESS
OF NOTCH DESIRED.
MAKE SEVERAL EACH OF
1/32", 1/16", etc.

COARSER
PAPER ON OTHER

WIDTH OF NOTCH

WHEN NOTCHING TRY EACH CUT BY
FITTING THE SPAR TO IT. IF NOT
PERFECTLY FLUSH, ADJUST CUT.

TOO SHALLOW | CUT SOME MORE

TOO DEEP | ADD SCRAP TO
NOTCH BOTTOM

PROFESSIONAL JOB! | TAKE A BOW!

METHOD TWO

NOTCHING RIBS BEFORE ASSEMBLY
ALMOST GUARANTEES POOR ALIGNMENT.
TO CURE IT...

MIS-CUT NOTCH CORRECT SPAR POSITION

RIB NOTCHED & GLUED IN

CUT OR SAND OUT

GLUE SPAR IN CORRECT POSITION

GLUE IN SCRAP →

METHOD THREE

NOTCH EACH RIB AND PIN IN PLACE OVER
PLAN. RIBS SHOULD BE FREE TO SLIDE
BACK & FORTH. LINE UP ALL NOTCHES BY
INSERTING SPARS.

CUT OFF FLUSH

FIT L.E. & T.E. TO GOOD STRAIGHT FIT BY SANDING OR CUTTING
RIB ENDS. IF GAPS OCCUR, FILL WITH SCRAP. DO **NOT** FORCE FIT!

L.E.

T.E.

CUT
OFF

L.E.

W-3

ADD

W-2

W-1

W-2 IS TOO LONG. TRIM
CAREFULLY TO FIT.

W-3 IS TOO
SHORT. GLUE
IN SCRAP & TRIM

L.E. SUPPOSED
TO FIT HERE

Three ways of avoiding wing wobbles.

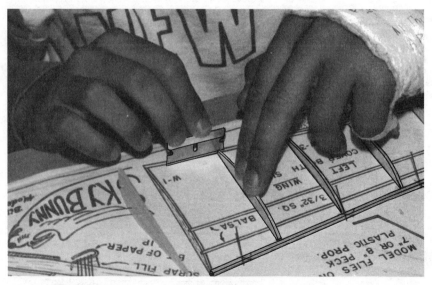

Trim the ribs you cut a bit long to length when they are in place.

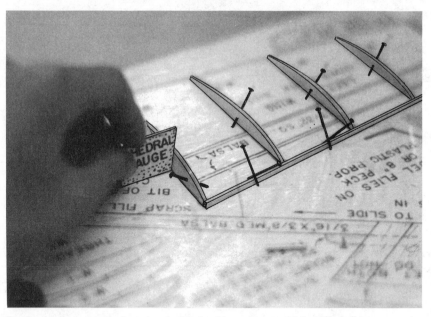

Pin the LE down to the board and add ribs. Note the use of the dihedral gauge on the root rib (W-1).

notch locations, and mark either the front or back of each notch over the location on the plan as you sight straight down on it. Then work your notching tool like a saw over each location until it is deep enough to accept the spar. Check the fit with a bit of ³/₃₂-inch scrap. Now glue in the spars. They can hang over the ends a bit and be trimmed off later.

The use of the dihedral gauge will give
you the right lean on the root rib (W-1).

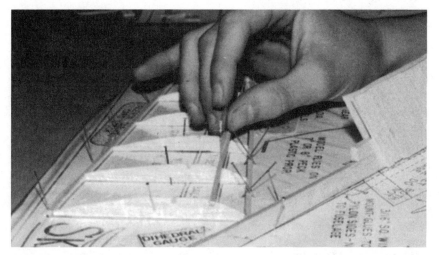

Mark the places where the spar passes over with a razor blade, and then cut notches
for the spar.

The second way to make a wing is the one most used over the years
by millions of modelers. This way involves making all the notches in the
rib first and then assembling them, usually all out of line, with the spar
snaking back and forth to connect them all. This is a rather clumsy way to
do it because the notches have to be lengthened at one edge or the other
to permit the spar to go straight. Then you have to fill in the extra bit of
notch with scrap.

The third way, which is a variation of the second, is to assemble the
ribs on the spar instead of the LE. This lines up all the notches so you can
trim the ends of the ribs to line up at the LE and TE ends over the plan.
This works best if you cut the ribs a little long, as I mentioned before.
Never bend the LE, TE, or spar to fit if you can help it, as bending not
only puts some strain into the wing, which might cause warps later, but it
looks crude. I prefer method one, which requires un-notched ribs to start
with.

There are two ways to glue up your wing. I prefer to get the glue in between the pieces being assembled. Some guys like to pin it all together dry and then wipe a little glue fillet at each joint. Both ways work.

Before your wing dries, double check to make sure that all the ribs are down flat touching the building board. If you don't do this, you'll have to cut high ribs out later and reglue them correctly. It's much easier to do it now! Also make sure all the spars are staying down in their little notches. One last caution: Don't try to use glue to fill gaps. If you cut a rib too short, either make a new one or glue some scrap in the gap. Good craftsmen fix problems, they don't try to slobber over them with glue or tissue!

BUILDING THE TAIL

Get in the habit of noticing how parts meet each other. The way the LE of the stab is done is a good example of the things some modelers miss. One of the sticks of the LE should cross the other where they form a ''V,'' not just butt together. This gives a little more gluing area than just a butt joint where their ends meet. Notice where each of the sticks starts and stops (lines on the plan tell the story), and cut them accordingly. Pin them down using the X-ing method.

THE WING AND PYLON SLIDER ASSEMBLY

Each pylon side is made of two pieces. If you are using printed kit parts, there should be no problem lining up the images. If you are using iron-on or thinner-transfer methods, no problem. If not, then study the pieces carefully to make sure everything lines up as the plan's side view shows, with the highest part of the pylon towards the front to give the wing an *angle of attack* needed to get lift. Test-fit the pylon side you made over the plan to see if it is done right. Mark an arrow facing forward if you have unprinted wood so you won't forget.

THE NOSE

Glue the three ''S'' pieces together, with the grain of the center one cross-ways of the other two for strength (plywood.) Glue them to the front of the fuselage stick as shown on the plan. **Note**: Make sure that the big end is forward so the thrust line points down. Glue it on the other way around and you have upthrust, which will give you a nice loop under power and hit you in the back of the head.

You will remember that I mentioned down thrust in chapter 1? Remember to respect the size tube and wire I used, as I allowed for the looseness of the shaft in the tube as shown. A nice, snug fit would be better unless you hit something and bent the shaft inside the tube. Then it would not be so nice, binding up until it was straightened or replaced.

Gluing on the aluminum tube can be done with your Testors Green Tube or with five-minute epoxy, where you mix parts A and B together. The epoxy is stronger, but to get any in your eye is very dangerous. Never

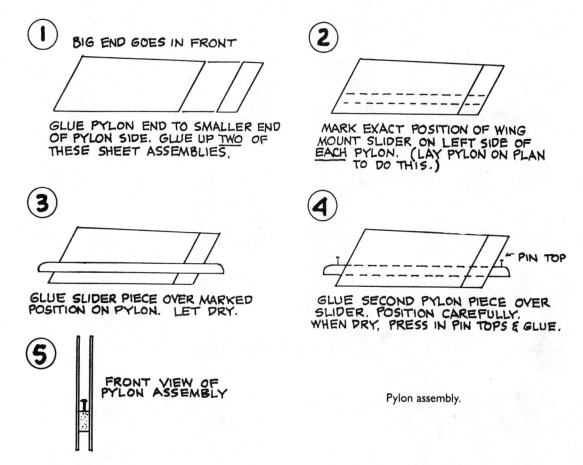

① BIG END GOES IN FRONT

GLUE PYLON END TO SMALLER END OF PYLON SIDE. GLUE UP TWO OF THESE SHEET ASSEMBLIES.

② MARK EXACT POSITION OF WING MOUNT SLIDER ON LEFT SIDE OF EACH PYLON. (LAY PYLON ON PLAN TO DO THIS.)

③ GLUE SLIDER PIECE OVER MARKED POSITION ON PYLON. LET DRY.

④ ← PIN TOP

GLUE SECOND PYLON PIECE OVER SLIDER. POSITION CAREFULLY. WHEN DRY, PRESS IN PIN TOPS & GLUE.

⑤ FRONT VIEW OF PYLON ASSEMBLY

Pylon assembly.

rub your eyes when you are working with chemicals of any kind. I have used hot-melt glue from a glue gun on occasion, and that works fairly well. Whatever you use, you will need to rough-up the outside diameter (OD) of the tube so the glue can get a grip on it. Use a file, your sanding block, or whatever—the rougher the better. Put a few wraps of thread around it and glue it on as shown on the plan. While the glue is drying, check it for sidethrust and to see if enough of it protrudes past the nose so the propeller won't hit anything. If it is not glued solidly, a crash will push the tube back, and your prop will stop against the front of the fuselage.

FINISHING THE WINGS AND TAIL FRAMES

First with your sanding block, and then with some fine sandpaper (220- or 320-grit), go around and even up all the parts so nothing stands out to snag the tissue later when you cover the model. Tissue will not cover up poor workmanship. It will just make a lot of wrinkles that will point at exactly what is causing them! If something comes apart while you are sanding, great! Better now than after it is covered, right? Glue it again and pin it down flat until it dries.

A rubber band hold the wing/pylon assembly on the fuselage for adjustment purposes. A short pin helps hook the rubber band on the wing slider.

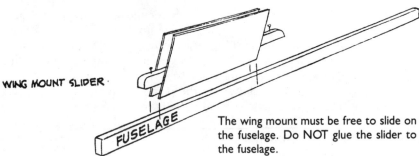

WING MOUNT SLIDER

FUSELAGE

The wing mount must be free to slide on the fuselage. Do NOT glue the slider to the fuselage.

The special shape a wing has given to it by the ribs is called an *airfoil*. The LE and TE need to be shaped with your sanding block (or a razor blade plane if you have one) to a nice, rounded section that blends in smoothly with the shape of the rib. It is easiest if you move the piece you are sanding right out to the edge of the table to give you some room to use your sanding block. Don't sand it too much, or you'll take away its strength. Sand just enough to blend in with the line of the rib shape.

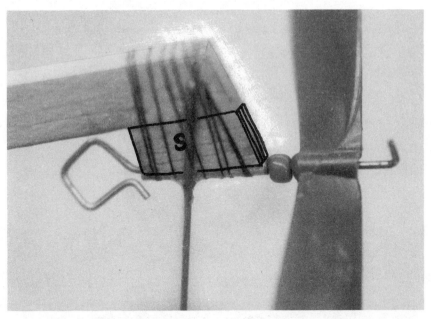

The three "S" pieces are glued together and cemented to the nose to hold the aluminum tube bearing. Note the glass bead. Make sure the thickest part of the "S" assembly is forward to give down thrust.

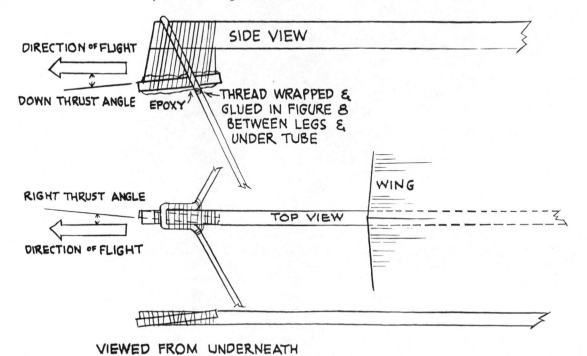

DIRECTION OF FLIGHT

SIDE VIEW

DOWN THRUST ANGLE

EPOXY

THREAD WRAPPED & GLUED IN FIGURE 8 BETWEEN LEGS & UNDER TUBE

RIGHT THRUST ANGLE

WING

TOP VIEW

DIRECTION OF FLIGHT

VIEWED FROM UNDERNEATH

Why down thrust?

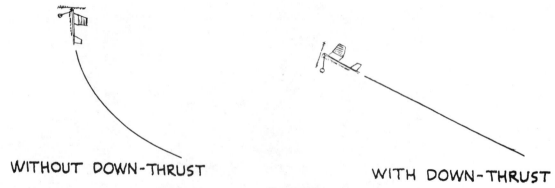

WITHOUT DOWN-THRUST   WITH DOWN-THRUST

Down thrust prevents "zoom" under high power.

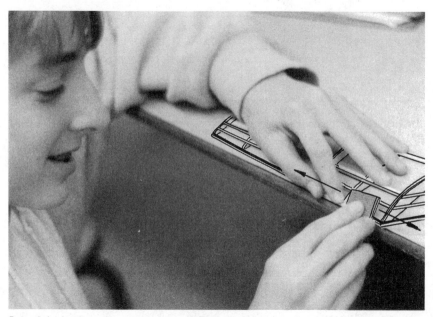

Round the leading edge with a sanding block. This is easiest done on the edge of a table or building board.

You can glue both the right and left wings together now, which will make for a nice, strong glue joint, or you can cover them first, which will make for a nicer covering job. Whichever you do, just make sure to measure the proper dihedral angle (4 inches under one wing tip with the other wing flat on the board). Make readjustments to the root ribs by cutting them loose and regluing if they do not fit well. It is important that the spars on one wing are glued to the spars on the other for strength. If they don't meet, either rebuild the center section so that they do, or lose strength there. You can brush acetone or dope thinner on Testors glue joints until they dissolve if repairs are needed.

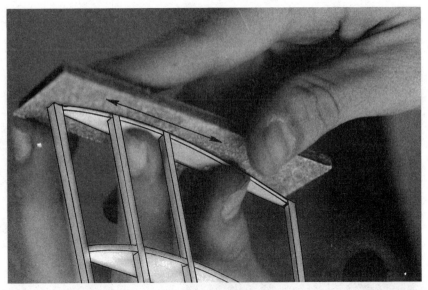

Make sure the root rib is sanded level as well as the rest of the wing structure.

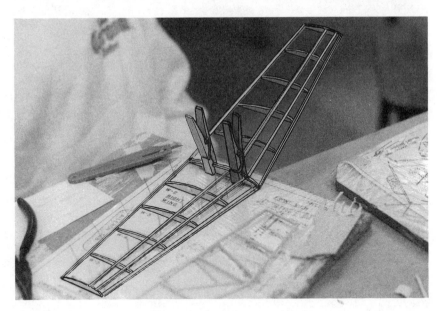

Glue the wing halves together.

A BIT MORE ON DIHEDRAL

Remember why we use dihedral? Lateral stability, right? Well, there are a lot of things happening. Because your prop is spinning right, the rubber wants to spin the model to which it is anchored in the opposite direction (left), which induces a left turn. Now is when the pylon comes in. The

Here the Sky Bunny's "bones" are tacked togther to check fit. The control tabs are not usually added until after covering has been completed.

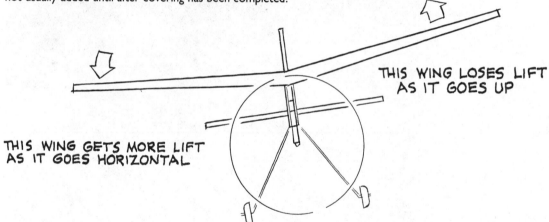

THIS WING LOSES LIFT
AS IT GOES UP

THIS WING GETS MORE LIFT
AS IT GOES HORIZONTAL

When a model banks in a turn, dihedral helps pick up the low wing.

corkscrew of air being thrown back by the propeller (*airscrew*) coming rearward and around the fuselage pushes on the left side of the pylon, which makes the model want to go right! The torque is usually a big factor in left turn, and the pylon helps control it, as does the effect of the right thrust that we built into the nose. Slight warps and tab adjustments also affect the model's turn, but 98 percent of the time you can be sure that your model will turn while flying—which is a very desirable thing. Otherwise, it would fly straight off the field, out of *thermals* (rising warm air that makes for long and high flights) and into walls if you are flying indoors!

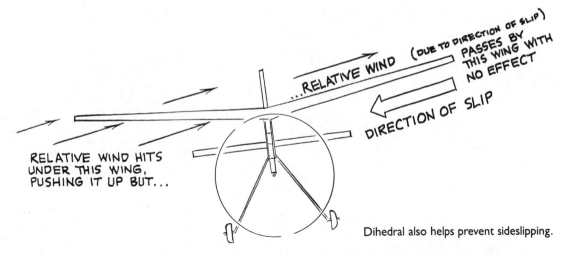

RELATIVE WIND (DUE TO DIRECTION OF SLIP) PASSES BY THIS WING WITH NO EFFECT

DIRECTION OF SLIP

RELATIVE WIND HITS UNDER THIS WING, PUSHING IT UP BUT...

Dihedral also helps prevent sideslipping.

When your model is in a turn, however, there is a tendency for the model to lose lift and begin to head earthward as the wing becomes less and less horizontal in a bank. (A completely vertical wing is not giving lift toward the sky anymore!) The wing on the inside of a tight turn is giving a lot less lift than the one on the outside of the turn, as it is moving slower, too. To regain this lift, dihedral is added. With dihedral, the wing on the inside of a turn gets more horizontal, giving *more* lift, while the wing on the outside goes up and *loses* lift, thereby helping level the airplane automatically.

If the model is sideslipping, the wing that the plane is slipping toward will have more air hitting its underside in sort of a sideways angle of attack, and it will be pushed up a bit, while the opposite wing will have a downward push on it to a degree. There are a lot of things involved—such as the amount of side area on the fuselage and where it is in relation to the wing, etc.—but for now, make your model like the plan. Don't leave out the dihedral! Yes, I know many full-sized airplanes don't have it, but they have pilots aboard to make corrections.

Chapter **3**

Finishing and flying

One of the hardest things about making more advanced model aircraft is making the bends in music wire for prop shafts and landing gear. Music wire, often called piano wire, is used in musical instruments to produce sound and is a rather hard steel that resists cutting and bending. A good way to learn to bend is to practice on something softer, such as copper wire or paper clips. Most bends can be made with common slip-joint or needle-nosed pliers, but a bending jig made from a piece of wood and a couple of nails or screws can be helpful. Bending jigs are cheap and quickly made. We will make two, one for the landing gear and one for the prop shaft.

The cut-off nails on the prop shaft jig are just close enough together to let the wire slip between them. The landing gear jig has bending posts about 1/2 inch apart. When the wire is going to be bent all the way around a post to form a prop hook or to come back in the same direction as it started, the bending post can be made the same size as the dimension needed. A 3/16-inch-diameter hook can be bent around a 3/16-inch-diameter screw and so on. Cutting the heads off makes the bent parts easier to remove.

BENDING THE LANDING GEAR

When I started making the Sky Bunny with an after-school group of junior-high kids, we had no idea of the exact problems that would arise. The biggest one was bending the wire. I had chosen .046-inch-diameter music wire to help make the design "bullet proof." This heavy wire would take up a lot of the shock of a bad landing. The only problem was that the kids couldn't bend it using pliers! Putting the twisting force sideways on the pliers would not do the job. Hence the bending jig.

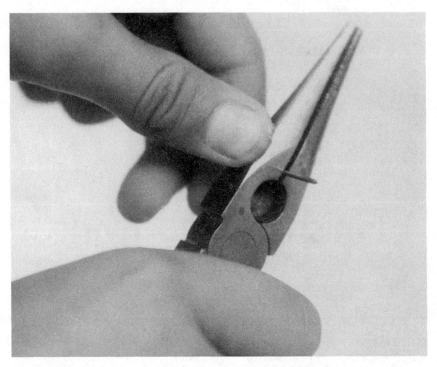

When bending music wire, grasps the wire as far down in the jaws as possible.

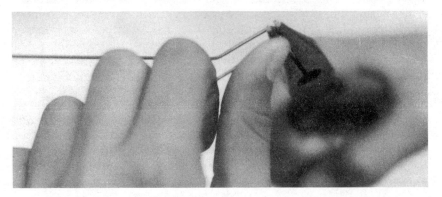

Bend the wire against back pressure from your thumb to prevent bowing.

The first thing to do is to mark off where the bends are supposed to be. I usually grab the wire at the place where I am going to bend it and, holding it over the pattern on the plan, grasp it with pliers right up against my fingers, which have "marked" the correct spot. I then bend it a little, holding it back over the plan to see if it was right before finishing the bend, making any necessary adjustments. The kids had a hard time getting it anywhere close, and the bends were definitely not all in the same plane.

The dictionary defines *plane* as ". . . without elevations or depressions; even; level; flat." That means when you have finished bending your landing-gear wire and you lay it on the table, all parts of it will touch the table at the same time. Sound easy? Well, I have seen grown men cry trying to get a bent-up part to come out with all surfaces in the same plane. The jig method can help here, because the surface of the board you are using is a flat plane.

Knowing exactly where the bend should be is easier if you mark the bend locations on the wire and check it over the plan after each bend, making a tiny part of the bend first and then checking location before you commit to the full, deep bend. Little "test bends" will come out easily, but once you bend it too far, bending it back can snap it off due to metal fatigue. Marks do not show up well on wire. You could use a paint pen, but a couple of wraps of masking tape around the wire at each location is easier. You can mark on the tape with a pen.

Look at the diagrams and you'll notice that I have given names to the landing gear sections to make them easier to discuss. The place the wheel fits (axle), I have called the *foot*. The long strut that goes from there up to the fuselage is the *leg*, and the part that goes up, over, and back down on the fuselage fit is the *saddle* or *crossover*.

You should note that all the dimensions I have laid out in the diagram are measured from the same place, the end of the wire. Measuring from each bend to the next is not good practice. If you make a tiny error at each place, you might be way off by the time you get to the other end.

Bend number 1 will be the easiest because it does not have to line up with anything. Check the bend to see if it is the correct angle by holding it over the plan and use your pliers to make minor changes. When you make bend number 2, you will have to make sure that the foot you have just formed is lying in the same plane—that is, flat against the surface of the bending jig. Have someone hold it down flat on the board if you need to use both hands. You could do this bend with needle-nose pliers if the wire wasn't so hard.

Sometimes heating the wire over the stove until it is red hot will make it easy to bend. However, it is dangerous to handle anything when it is red hot, and sometimes the wire can become brittle when it cools.

When you have finished all the bends, cut off the excess wire. This can be fun because you can ruin cheap cutting edges with the hardened wire. Making a nick with the corner of a file and bending it back and forth with pliers until it snaps off can do the job, as long as you remember to clean up any sharp ends with the file. Very hard wire can also ruin a file, though, so be warned. I prefer to use a Dremel Moto-Tool with a #409 cut-off wheel. This is one of the handiest things in the workshop, but it should be used with safety glasses or a face shield. Grinding anything or even snipping off ends of the wire with pliers can endanger your eyes. Always be careful—no model is worth losing an eye. By the way, if you just *can't* bend .046-inch music wire, go ahead and use .031-inch; it will just be floppier. You could even fly the Sky Bunny without landing gear, but then it would no longer be an R.O.G. model.

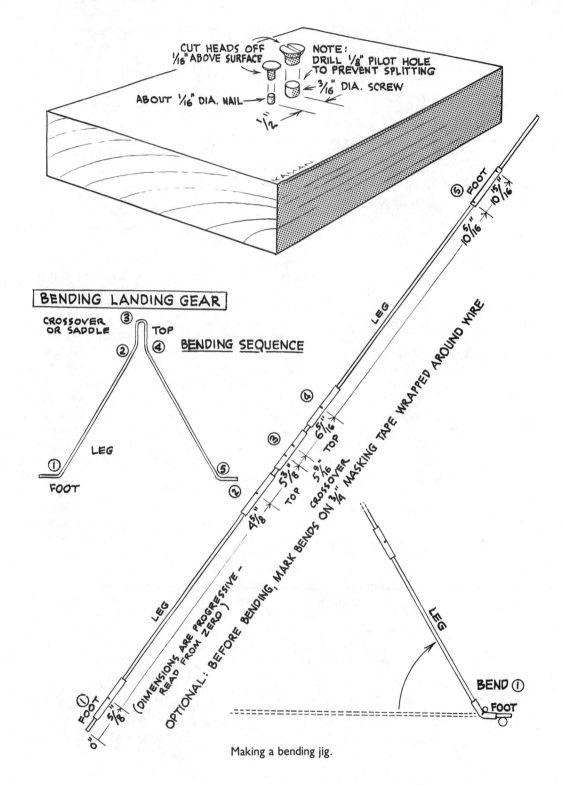

CUT HEADS OFF
1/16" ABOVE SURFACE

NOTE:
DRILL 1/8" PILOT HOLE
TO PREVENT SPLITTING

3/16" DIA. SCREW

ABOUT 1/16" DIA. NAIL →

1/2"

BENDING LANDING GEAR

CROSSOVER
OR SADDLE   ③   TOP
②   ④   **BENDING SEQUENCE**

LEG

①   LEG

FOOT   ⑤   ②

FOOT   ⑤

⑤ FOOT   15/16"   10/16"

LEG

MASKING TAPE WRAPPED AROUND WIRE

④

③   6 5/16"   TOP

5 3/8"   5 9/16"   TOP
TOP   CROSSOVER

4 5/8"

LEG

(DIMENSIONS ARE PROGRESSIVE –
READ FROM ZERO)

OPTIONAL: BEFORE BENDING, MARK BENDS ON 3/4" MASKING TAPE WRAPPED AROUND WIRE

LEG

BEND ①

FOOT

① FOOT   5/8"

0"

Making a bending jig.

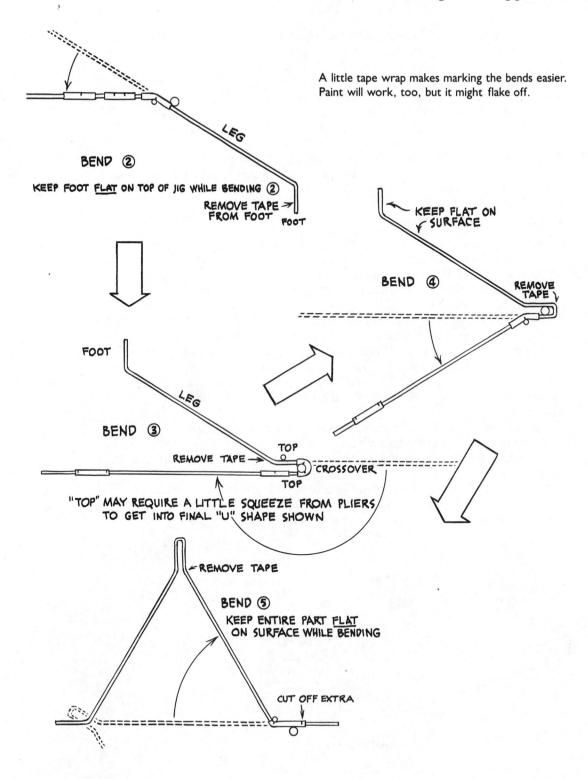

A little tape wrap makes marking the bends easier. Paint will work, too, but it might flake off.

LEG

BEND ②

KEEP FOOT FLAT ON TOP OF JIG WHILE BENDING ②

REMOVE TAPE FROM FOOT

FOOT

KEEP FLAT ON SURFACE

BEND ④

REMOVE TAPE

FOOT

LEG

BEND ③

REMOVE TAPE

TOP

TOP

CROSSOVER

"TOP" MAY REQUIRE A LITTLE SQUEEZE FROM PLIERS TO GET INTO FINAL "U" SHAPE SHOWN

REMOVE TAPE

BEND ⑤

KEEP ENTIRE PART FLAT ON SURFACE WHILE BENDING

CUT OFF EXTRA

If your wheels will not fit the size wire you have used, drill the holes bigger (a red-hot wire can be used if you are careful). If the hole is too big, you can *bush* it by drilling oversize to allow an aluminum tube bearing to be pushed in. A rolled-and-glued paper tube or a bit of hardwood drilled to the right axle size can be glued in the wheel. Hold the wheel on by making a little nick near the end of the axle using a file or cut-off wheel, and then wind some thread around until you have a little ball locked onto the notch. Use glue on the thread while you are winding. Sometimes wheels with large holes can work themselves around the first bend and up the leg. If this happens, you might want to do a thread ball on the inside of the axle, too.

BENDING THE PROPELLER SHAFT

The prop shaft can be bent with needle-nose pliers in a diamond shape, with the ends squared off. The trick is to make sure the part where the rubber will hook on is directly opposite the shaft that goes to the propeller. If it is not, there will be a whole lot of shakin' goin' on as the off-center rubber hook whips around!

Spin the finished shaft between your fingers to make sure the hook is centered. Also, check it on a flat surface to make sure the hook is in the same plane as the shaft proper. While you are at it, make a couple of extra shafts. Use the best one, and take the rest with you to the flying field along with the pliers, just in case you bend one. It is hard to straighten them on the plane, and the end usually snaps off when you bend the end down to get the prop off.

A classy way to finish off the prop hook on the shaft is to shove a bit of plastic insulation from electric wiring or a piece of small plastic tubing over it. A little saliva helps it slip on. You could also use heat-shrink tubing. It helps save the rubber a bit from being cut by the wire.

Making a jig-bent shaft is about the same. The "bend-back" on the last bend is necessary to center up the hook with the shaft. Again, check by twirling it between your fingers to see that the center of the eye lines up.

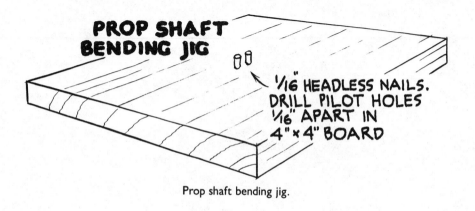

Prop shaft bending jig.

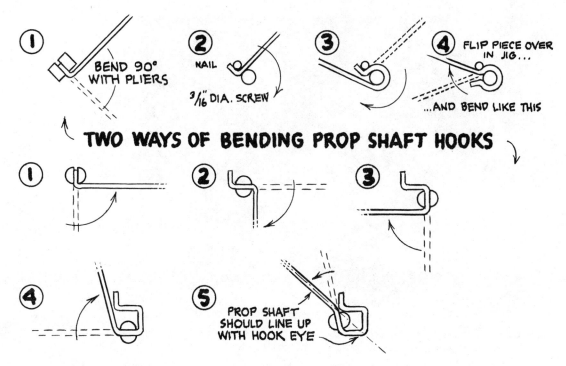

TWO WAYS OF BENDING PROP SHAFT HOOKS

You can use either the homemade jig or needle-nose pliers to bend the prop shaft hooks.

COVERING

Both sides of the wing get covered, but only one side of the tail parts. This is to save weight. One ounce of weight in the tail means adding five on the nose to balance it because the tail has more leverage, so keep the tail light.

It helps to pre-shrink the tissue for the tail surfaces because they are thin and easily warped. I usually cut a hole out of a cardboard box a bit smaller than the piece of tissue I want to shrink and then glue the tissue over it with white glue. When it is dry, I spray the tissue with a fine water mist from an old hair-spray bottle. This will shrink the tissue on the box, not on the model, and hopefully save you from warp problems later. The Sky Bunny wing should be strong enough to resist non-pre-shrunk tissue, but you can pre-shrink all of your tissue if you want to be on the safe side.

If you haven't glued the wings together yet at the roots, make sure they match up. Did you round all the LEs and TEs to blend in with the shape of the airfoil? Do a final sanding with 320- or 400-grit abrasive paper to make sure everything is smooth, especially the top edges of the ribs where they will touch the tissue.

Use a separate sheet of tissue for the top of each wing and also for the bottom (4 pieces). The grain of the tissue should run *spanwise* (the long way) of the wing. Find the grain by tearing a corner of the sheet. It tears

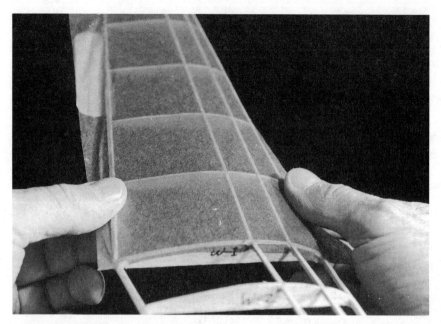

Cover the top of the wing first using thinned-out white glue. Pull the wrinkles out with your thumbs, keeping them dry so the tissue will not stick to them.

easiest with the grain. Whatever you do, don't try to wrap the tissue around the wing from top to bottom . . . it usually doesn't make for a neat job.

Attach the tissue by painting around the frame you are covering with white glue thinned out—60% glue, 40% water. Lower the tissue carefully onto it and pull the wrinkles out along the edges with your thumbs. Wipe your thumbs often so the tissue won't stick to them and tear. Cover the top first (it's the hardest), and let it dry. If you mess up your first try, don't give up. It takes practice.

Trim the excess tissue off along the edges using a new single-edged razor blade or use your sanding block to sand at the LE and TE. Now cover the bottom and trim off the excess tissue. If you want to make sure that the raw balsa does not show, you can cover the top last, cut the excess off to within about 1/8 inch or less from the edges, and wrap that around to hide the edge. Make cuts out from the corners to permit overlap at tip and root. If you don't want to do that, it will still fly, and a little cover-up with a felt pen around the edge will do wonders. Yellow tissue and felt pen match nicely.

The tissue can be shrunk right on the wing, using rubbing alcohol with some water in it—either sprayed or put on with a soft brush. The more water, the tighter it will get. The wing is pretty strong on this plane, so you should not have the same problem you would with the tail surfaces, which are much thinner and require pre-shrunk tissue.

While it is not essential, a little card stock at the center section adds strength.

Trim off excess tissue with a new razor blade. Cut away from your fingers while holding the wing.

Note: If you glued the wing halves together before covering, be sure you cover each upper half of the wing with a separate sheet of tissue. Tissue will not make the bend at the center while it is also fitting the camber—too much stretch! You will need to make a little longer piece than you need and do "cut-and-try" at the wing root ribs, cutting the end of the sheet at a slight curvature to follow the line of the root rib from LE to TE.

DOPE

The liquid plastic paint used on the tissue is called dope. They use it on full-sized fabric-covered planes, too. The most popular type with rubber modelers is *nitrate* dope. It goes on nicely and does not add much weight. With colored tissue, clear dope is best because colored dope weighs more and makes the tissue harder to patch when it gets tears.

There are two types of nitrate dope: *tautening* and *non-tautening*. For a light structure, you will want the non-tautening variety so as not to warp your wing when it shrinks. In the old days all nitrate dope was the tautening type, and a "plasticizer" such as castor oil, oil of wintergreen, or TCP (tricresylphosphate) was added at the rate of 5 to 10 drops per ounce. Some modelers still go that route. When glow engines using an alcohol-based fuel came along in the late 1940s, butyrate dope came into wide use because it resisted this fuel. Butyrate dope is not a pleasure to brush on, and I recommend that you avoid it.

Today, most of the dope in hobby shops is acrylic-based or other funny stuff that keeps changing each time you buy it. A quart of non-tautening nitrate clear and a quart of thinner are excellent investments for a beginning modeler, and they will last you a very long time. You are going to mix the dope 50/50 with thinner, so you will probably run out of thinner first. Aircraft supply stores have it, as do many of the model suppliers mentioned in the back of this book.

The SIG Lite Coat dope is the only other dope I have had good non-shrink results with. SIG's nitrate dope actually loosened the silk covering job on one of my models, so if you have gotten something too tight and twisted up, you might try that! (I think they must have over-plasticized it!) About two coats of 50/50 dope should be plenty.

Applying the dope

An old baby-food bottle is good for mixing small quantities of dope and thinner. You can apply dope as it comes out of the can or bottle, but it will be thick and won't cover evenly. Be sure to use dope with plenty of ventilation and not around flames or gas water heaters. Put down plenty of newspapers—not only on the bench where you are working, but on the floor, too. I've spilled dope on nice floors often enough to know that no matter how careful you are, there is still that chance of ruining something. Use about a 1/2-inch-wide artist's flat brush. Use a cheap one at your own risk; they will shed bristles constantly. When in doubt, ask for a recommendation at an art store.

Dip the brush into the dope about halfway or so up on the bristles. Then, as you take it out of the jar, wipe the dope off one side of the brush on the edge so it runs back inside. Keep the full side up to prevent drips. Hold the wing so the long dimension is in line with your forearm.

Start at the center and apply the dope, using a twisting motion of your wrist and forearm, back and forth. Do not push the brush back and forth away from and towards your body. You have little control that way, and it is tiring. Overlap your strokes.

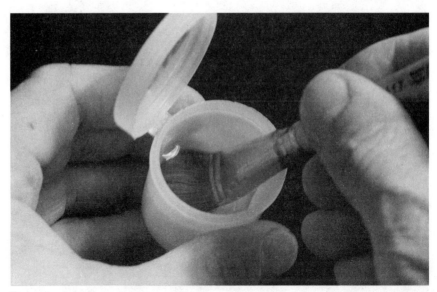

Snap-top plastic containers are useful for small quantities of model dope. Always use dope in a well-ventilated place. It's powerful stuff!

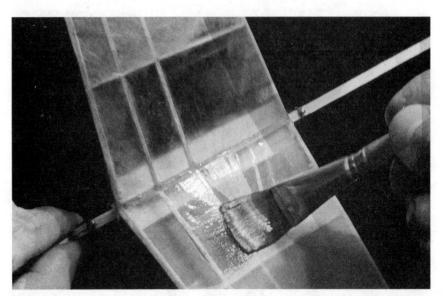

Flow the thinned dope onto the tissue with overlapping strokes. Do not keep going back over the same area. Hold the wing so that the light reflects off the wet dope to show you what you have missed.

Hold the wing so the light will shine off the doped surface to help you see if you are covering well or leaving dry places. If you see it leaving dry places, get more dope on the brush. Keeping the brush full and advancing out to the tip from the root with overlapping strokes across the

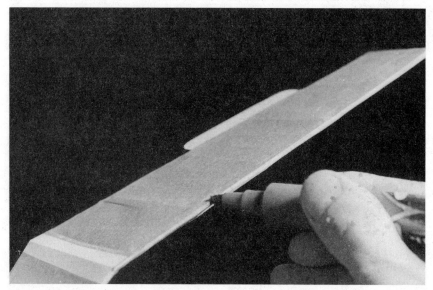

Raw balsa can be colored to matched tissue color if you wish. Yellow is the easiest.

After the wing has been glued on the pylon, add a little extra glue at the LE and TE areas for extra strength.

short dimension of the wing should do the trick. Flow the dope on; never try to massage it around with a fairly dry brush. Do both the top and bottom at the same sitting so they will dry and shrink up evenly.

Some modelers pin the dry-to-the-touch wings and tail parts down to the board and leave them overnight or more to set. One world champion even left his on the board for a *year* to make sure they were set and would not warp. If your wing or stab does warp, you can steam it over a teakettle (don't burn yourself!) and pin it down or at least twist it in the opposite direction while it cools and dries.

CLEANING UP

Wipe off the threads of the dope bottle and put a little Vaseline on them so you can get it off easily next time. If you forget this, you will probably need to invert the bottle and flow a little dope thinner or acetone in between the bottle and the cap and let it sit for a few minutes to loosen it.

I clean my brushes by "painting out" as much of the dope as I can on a piece of newspaper and them rinsing it in dope thinner. Then I wash it carefully in soap and warm water. A drop of Woolite on the bristles before shaping them for storage won't hurt. Some even wrap the bristle end in aluminum foil folded over to protect their investment. A good brush, well cared for, can outlast a dozen cheap ones and give you nice work each time.

PRE-FLIGHT CHECK

Book one of this series ("A Beginning Guide to Building the Peck R.O.G.") contained extensive basic pre-flight and flying instructions which should be reviewed if you have it. Knowing that some of you will have missed it, I'll zip through a few rather important points just in case!

It is essential that the model have the warps removed before trying to fly it. You can hold the model out at arm's length and close one eye and sight under the wing and tail parts to see if there are any twists. You can put the wing or stab halves on a flat table and see if any corner does not touch. If there is a warp, steam it out now. I often use a gas flame, keeping the wing well away from the fire and twisting it in the opposite direction from the warp. Hair driers can also be used, but steaming is the most permanent. Pinning it down flat and re-checking in a few minutes will tell you if your de-warping worked or not. A bit of washout in each wing (about .030 inch or the thickness of a credit card) might be good for the flight characteristics. In extreme cases, the wing might have to be re-covered after it has been stripped and soaked overnight in water and then pinned down flat for two weeks!

Also check the alignment of all the parts and all the glue joints. These things are easier to fix at home than on the field. Make up a rubber motor or two, chewing some saliva into the knots to make sure they can be pulled as tight as possible. Lubricate the motors by putting them in a resealable bag with a few drops of rubber lube. Put a drop of oil or two on the prop shaft so it spins easily. Check the free-wheeling notch where it contacts the bent-up end of the shaft, and make sure it is catching. If it isn't, carefully cut it a little deeper into the prop hub (center).

If you don't have a rubber winder (available from Peck or other suppliers), you might want to use a hand drill with a bent nail hook installed.

The Fiskars drill is a good one, and it is available in many hardware stores. The head of your nail hook should be behind the chuck jaws so it won't come out while you are winding the rubber motor. A cardboard box to carry your model in with a removable top that is not going to come down and crush your model is a good idea. Never carry it in a sack! Carry the heavy stuff to the field in a separate container so the model won't be damaged by loose pliers, winder, bottle of rubber lube, etc. Take extra rubber, prop shafts, glue, some scrap balsa and tissue for repairs, and a copy of the troubleshooting chart in this book!

AT THE FIELD

Find a large field with grass and no trees or houses nearby (Lots of luck!). Don't try to fly in the wind. Early morning or just before dark are often the best times. Give the model a quick look-over to make sure there are no warps that have crept back in on the way to the field due to temperature changes, humidity, or bad luck. Breathe heavily (for moisture) on any warped surfaces, and twist in the other direction. This usually will hold it for a while. Check before each flight.

For a test flight, you might want to use a rubber motor of a smaller rubber size or at least longer than recommended to give low power. Never test with a short or very powerful motor (it runs the winds out too fast at high speed, making any crashes worse). The technique of *trimming* the model (making small adjustments to make the flight better) is to start with low-power, only-half-wound flights and work up to full power when the model shows that it can handle it. Minor misalignments or warps become major at high speeds.

Starting with the wing fairly far forward, test under low power. Here, Ed Arteaga, a student in one of my aeronautics classes, shows the correct launch angle for a test flight.

Hook your rubber motor on the propeller hook and have a friend hold the rubber in place there with a hand over the prop to keep it from turning. Hook your winder on the other end (with the knot) and begin winding in a clockwise direction, with the motor stretched out double its normal length. (Normal motor length is usually a loop 1¹/₂ times as long as the distance between the places it hooks on, or about an 18-inch loop of ³/₁₆-inch flat rubber for the Sky Bunny.)

Before you launch, check to see that the trim tabs are all neutral and not bent. If you want to hand-launch the model, hold it at the center of gravity under the wing with your right hand, and hold the prop in your left (reverse this if you are left-handed). Wait for a calm period, if there is a wind. You can launch into a light wind, but if it is blowing enough to flap a flag and you are determined to fly, you might try an otherwise non-recommended downwind launch to prevent a wind-induced stall.

Let the prop go for about 3 seconds before you give the plane a light toss forward. Don't aim it up at a high angle, and don't throw it! You must now be a good observer, and note two things—Did it go up or down, and did it go right or left? (Remember these directions are as seen from the cockpit.) You won't know what to change before the next flight unless you pay attention.

TRIM TABS

The card stock tabs that you glued on the TE of the wings, stab, and rudder are used to make flight adjustments. If the model went very tight to the left and dropped the left wing, then you'd want to open up the turn a bit by bending the rudder tab to the right about the thickness of credit card for a start. Bending the aileron tab on the left wing down about .050 inch (thickness of a dime) will help that wing gain lift and open up the turn.

The Sky Bunny takes off under high power (note the slight left torque roll) and then goes into its right climb circle.

The model is clearly in its right climb pattern five seconds after R.O.G. and is heading up and away!

If the spiral dive left was steep, maybe even bending the elevator tab on the stab up about .030 inch would help. The safest way to make adjustments is to do only one thing at a time so you know what its effect was. If you bend in up elevator and down left aileron at the same time, how will you know which one made the difference on the next flight? Keep testing, gradually building up to full winds as the flights improve to the point of no stalls, no dives, and a nice wide circling flight.

The Sky Bunny is a trainer, so experiment with different adjustments to see how they affect the flight path. Try moving the wing forward or *aft* (rearward) to see what that does. An ideal flight is a wide, climbing right turn which was designed into the model (pylon, right thrust). If the model dives, you can move the wing forward, which will make the tail moment longer (making the tail heavier in relation to the nose, and the angle of attack at which the model flies will be increased, giving more lift). The angle of attack of the wing can also be changed, by adding a $1/32$-inch *shim* (spacing piece) between the front of the pylon slider and the fuselage, giving more lift. A stall might be cured by shimming at the rear, decreasing the angle of attack and giving less lift.

Consult the troubleshooting chart often until you know by heart what is causing each problem. Have fun with your Sky Bunny, and if it breaks, fix it instead of throwing it away. It will get better and better as you solve its problems. Wrecks are never as bad as they seem, and a model broken in ten places is a lot easier to put back in order than to build a new one!

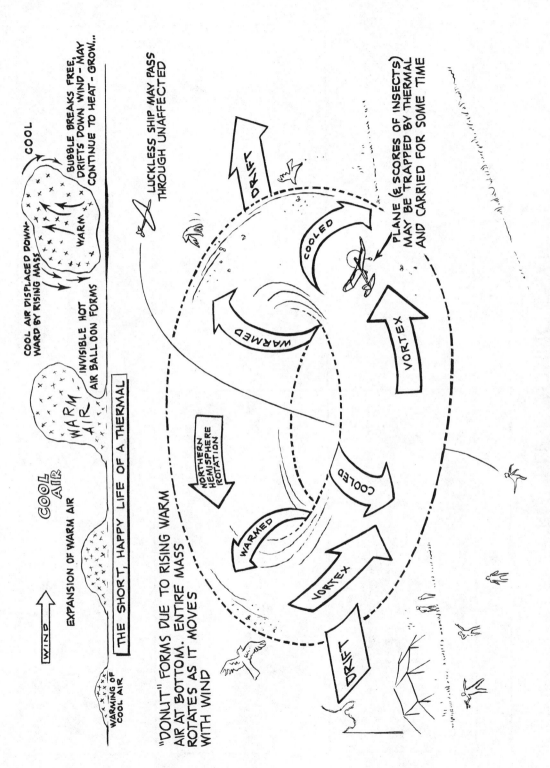

COOL

COOL AIR DISPLACED DOWN-
WARD BY RISING MASS

WARM

BUBBLE BREAKS FREE,
DRIFTS DOWN WIND – MAY
CONTINUE TO HEAT – GROW...

INVISIBLE HOT
AIR BALLOON FORMS

WARM
AIR

COOL
AIR

LUCKLESS SHIP MAY PASS
THROUGH UNAFFECTED

EXPANSION OF WARM AIR

WIND

WARMING OF
COOL AIR

THE SHORT, HAPPY LIFE OF A THERMAL

"DONUT" FORMS DUE TO RISING WARM
AIR AT BOTTOM. ENTIRE MASS
ROTATES AS IT MOVES
WITH WIND

DRIFT

COOLED

WARMED

NORTHERN
HEMISPHERE
ROTATION

COOLED

WARMED

VORTEX

VORTEX

DRIFT

PLANE (& SCORES OF INSECTS)
MAY BE TRAPPED BY THERMAL
AND CARRIED FOR SOME TIME

Flying your model into a thermal can stretch your flight and sometimes even keep it up longer than you'd like.

TROUBLESHOOTING CHART
No wind blowing; model launch normal

The Problem	What Might Fix It
 **NORMAL CLIMB** · **NORMAL GLIDE** · **DIVE** — Model dives straight in.	1. Bend the trailing edge of the stab or the elevator tab up .030 inches. 2. Add a bit of modeling clay about the size of half a pea to the tail. 3. As a last resort, reglue the wing 1/2" farther forward.
"ROLLER-COASTER" STALLS (PORPOISING) · **SEVERE STALL** — Model stalls (nose first goes up, hesitates slightly, then drops to a dive; roller-coaster).	1. Bend the trailing edge of the stab or the elevator down .030 inches. 2. If the model wasn't turning, bend the rear of the rudder or the rudder tab about .030 inches left (as seen from the rear). 3. Try a bit of modeling clay about the size of a pea on the nose, as far forward as it will go.
Model refuses to fly left, even though you try everything. 	1. Go with the flow—fly right. Why fight it? You might have built it as a RH model without knowing it.

RIGHT DIVE:

1. Hold the model at arm's length. Close one eye and see if the wings are warped. The right wing should be untwisted, but the left should have about .070 inches wash-in. If too much wash-in, breathe on it and twist in opposite direction. Recheck.
2. Bend rear of rudder or tab about .030 inches to the left.
3. Bend the trailing edge of the stab up about .050 inches.
4. Add about a half a pea of clay to the tail.
5. Bend right aileron tab down .050 inches and left tab up .070 inches.

LEFT DIVE:

1. Hold the model at arm's length. Close one eye and see if the wings are warped. The right wing should be untwisted, but the left wing should have about .070 inches wash-in. If not enough wash-in, breathe on it and twist leading edge higher.
2. Bend rear of rudder or tab about .050 inches to the right.
3. Bend the trailing edge of the stab or elevator up about .050 inches.
4. Add about half a pea of modeling clay to the tail.
5. Bend left aileron tab down about .050 inches and right tab up .070 inches.

1. Remember that the rubber spinning the prop makes the plane roll left. When the motor runs down, this force is missing. Try adjusting the model so that it glides well, and then play with the prop-shaft part of the nose bearing. Twisting it a little right will open up a too-tight left turn; a little left will turn a straight climb into a left circle, etc.

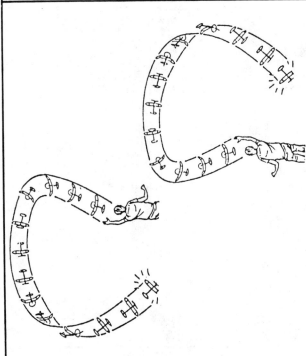

Spiral dive to the right: Model raises its left wing and finally crashes to the right. Spiral dive to the left: Model raises its right wing and finally crashes to the left.

The model flies great (power phases) until it runs out of power, then it dives, stalls, or goes straight.

PICK THE TWO HARDEST STICKS IN KIT TO USE FOR WING LEADING EDGES

3/32" SQ. HARD BALSA

W-8

3/32" SQUARE BALSA

COVER BOTH SIDES OF WINGS

LEFT WING

W-6   W-5   W-4   W-3   W-2   W-1

W-7

GLUE THREE S-1's TOGETHER

AILERON TAB (2) CARD STOCK

1/16" ALUMINUM TUBE

S-1

SIDE VIEW OF NOSE NOTE DOWN THRUST

BEST LOCATION ON WING ON FUSELAGE CAN ONLY BE DETERMINED BY FLIGHT TESTING. MODEL SHOULD HAVE A SMOOTH GLIDE WITHOUT STALLING OR DIVING.

WING

BOTTOM VIEW: NOTE RIGHT THRUST

P-1

3/16" SQ. BALSA

SKY BUNNY

P-2

WING MUST BE FREE TO SLIDE

GLASS BEAD OR BRASS WASHERS

BIND WITH THREAD

RUB ON TWO OR THREE GLUE SKINS

WRAP WITH THREAD AND GLUE

FRONT VIEW

WING

PYLON

P-3 and P-4

P-1 and P-2

.045" DIA. MUSIC WIRE LANDING GEAR

WING MOUNT GLUE TO PYLON SIDES

ALTERNATIVE FRONT END USING NYLON NOSE BEARING AND .041" DIA. PROP SHAFT. (GLUE IN RIGHT THRUST)

USE 1" DIA. PECK WHEELS

PROP SHAFT: 1/32" MUSIC WIRE

FUSELAGE: FITS BETWEEN PYLON SIDES,BUT IS NOT GLUED TO THEM

Sky Bunny plans. To achieve full-size plans, enlarge these pages 166%. Enlarge both pages, then attach them to form a single-sheet plan.

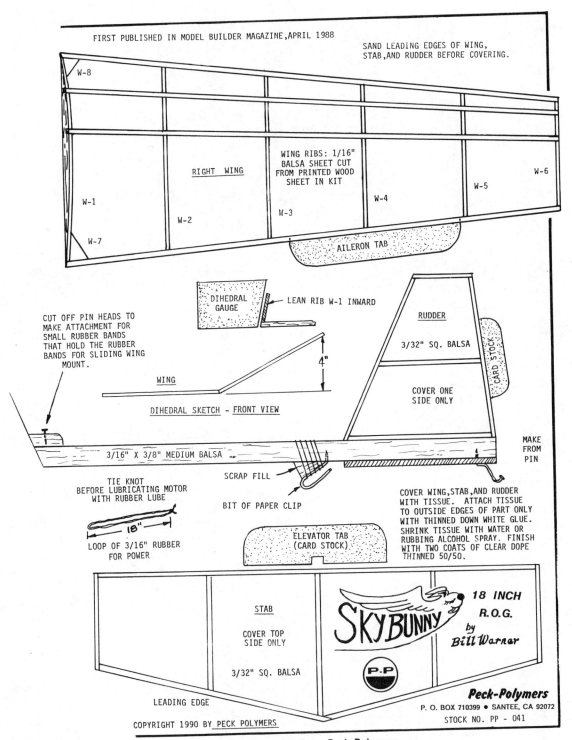

FIRST PUBLISHED IN MODEL BUILDER MAGAZINE, APRIL 1988

SAND LEADING EDGES OF WING, STAB, AND RUDDER BEFORE COVERING.

W-8

RIGHT WING

WING RIBS: 1/16" BALSA SHEET CUT FROM PRINTED WOOD SHEET IN KIT

W-1

W-2

W-3

W-4

W-5

W-6

W-7

AILERON TAB

DIHEDRAL GAUGE

LEAN RIB W-1 INWARD

CUT OFF PIN HEADS TO MAKE ATTACHMENT FOR SMALL RUBBER BANDS THAT HOLD THE RUBBER BANDS FOR SLIDING WING MOUNT.

RUDDER

3/32" SQ. BALSA

CARD STOCK

WING

4"

COVER ONE SIDE ONLY

DIHEDRAL SKETCH - FRONT VIEW

3/16" X 3/8" MEDIUM BALSA

MAKE FROM PIN

TIE KNOT BEFORE LUBRICATING MOTOR WITH RUBBER LUBE

SCRAP FILL

BIT OF PAPER CLIP

18"

LOOP OF 3/16" RUBBER FOR POWER

ELEVATOR TAB (CARD STOCK)

COVER WING, STAB, AND RUDDER WITH TISSUE. ATTACH TISSUE TO OUTSIDE EDGES OF PART ONLY WITH THINNED DOWN WHITE GLUE. SHRINK TISSUE WITH WATER OR RUBBING ALCOHOL SPRAY. FINISH WITH TWO COATS OF CLEAR DOPE THINNED 50/50.

STAB

COVER TOP SIDE ONLY

3/32" SQ. BALSA

SKYBUNNY

18 INCH R.O.G.

by Bill Warner

P-P

LEADING EDGE

Peck-Polymers

P. O. BOX 710399 ● SANTEE, CA 92072

STOCK NO. PP - 041

COPYRIGHT 1990 BY PECK POLYMERS

Kit available from Peck Polymers.

What is wrong with this picture? 1. The models are not flying and should be kept in a box. 2. The rubber motors should not be touching the ground. 3. Your rubber winder should never be left on the ground (step on it and find out why).

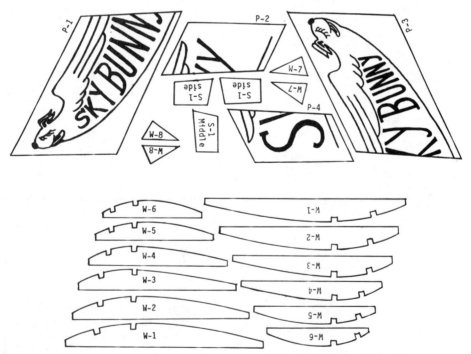

Printwood plans for the Sky Bunny. Enlarge 166% for full-size plans.

PRE-FLIGHT CHECK

 ①

ANYTHING LOOSE? GLUE IT!

②

ANY WARPS? STEAM 'EM OUT WHILE TWISTING IN OPPOSITE DIRECTION

RUDDER KICKED RIGHT OR LEFT?

③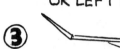

...OR   STAB NOT LEVEL? FIX 'EM!

④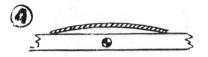

WING MOUNTED LIKE THIS

...NOT THIS

... OR THIS

⑤

STAB MOUNTED OK? THIS "BOOM" ANGLE OK, TOO

NOT LIKE THIS

OR THIS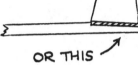

⑥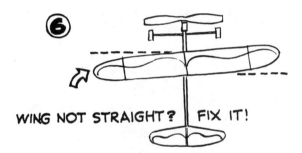

WING NOT STRAIGHT?   FIX IT!

Appendix

Suppliers & Publications

*E*verything covered in this book is available from Peck Polymers as a convenience for modelers living away from good sources of modeling materials. Also listed are other suppliers who carry the same types of useful kits, plans, and supplies. Actual prices will probably be higher than those quoted here. Always send an SASE (self-addressed, stamped envelope) when requesting information. Many of these sources operate on a shoestring! Sending cash through the mail is never advised. A check or a postal money order is better. A more complete list will be included with Book Three of this series, where more advanced projects are covered.

SUPPLIERS

A. A. Lidberg Plans
614 E. Fordham
Tempe, AZ 85283

Lidberg has many "profile" model plans that are tissue-covered and easy to build. He has more advanced plans, too, with excellent instruction sheets.

Allen Hunt Plan Service
PO Box 726
Dunbar, WV 25064-0726

Allen has over 2,000 plans, many with line drawings in the catalog so you can get an idea what they look like. A good many of the old-time model plans have been redone with rib and former outlines and both wings.

(Sometimes old plans lack one wing because the old practice was to rub oil on the plan so the wing outline would be visible for building on the back side. Rib outlines were often printed on the kit wood instead of on the plans, so this is a good feature Allen has added.) Some plans have three-view scale drawings included. Catalog $3.00, refundable with order.

Blue Ridge Model Products
Box 329
Skyland, NC 28776

Good model kits for beginners with some of the work done for you. Wood is excellent. One of my students got a nine-minute thermal flight with one of the beginner's hand-launched glider kit models. Catalog $0.50.

Champion Model Products
880 Carmen Court
La Verne, CA 91750

Rubber strip by the pound and advanced competition kits for rubber in Coupe D'Hiver, Mulvihill, and Wakefield classes. Catalog $1.50.

Easy Built Models
Box 1059
Beamsville, Ontario LOR 1BO
CANADA

Large selection of model kits, plans, and supplies from the "good ol' days." Prices are reasonable, and the kits range from quite simple to complex. Some of the designs are a bit primitive by today's standards, and the wood might not always be what you would wish to use, but despite this, they have some interesting stuff. For $2.00, you can get their list of kits and an interesting booklet called *Facts and Building Tips*.

Peck Polymers
Box 710399
Santee, CA 92072
Telephone: (619) 448-1818 Fax: (619) 448-1833

This is the one-stop source for the stuff used in this book. It is highly recommended. Model for model, Peck has more winners than any other manufacturer I know. The Sky Bunny kit is available from Peck, as are the model projects covered in Books 1 and 3 of this series. Their line of really good kits, supplies, and plans is second to none for the beginning modeler, though you probably would not be interested in their RC blimps just yet! Their extensive and fascinating catalog is $3.00. If you would like just a listing of the models we use, send a large SASE and ask for the "Hey Kid!" list for free.

MODEL MAGAZINES

Model Aviation
1810 Samuel Morse Drive
Reston, VA 22090

This is the official publication of the Academy of Model Aeronautics, the organization that controls most model airplane activity in the U.S. Besides the magazine, members get contest rule books, liability insurance, and representation in Washington. I have written the Free-Flight Scale column in this magazine, which covers all phases of airplane modeling, for the past dozen years. The monthly magazine is $29.00 per year ($10.00 for schools and $13.50 for libraries) or comes free with the membership. Membership is $40.00 per year for those over 19 by July 1; $16.00 for kids not yet 19 by July 1; and $21.00 for the over-65 crowd. (First-time members submit proof of age.)

Model Builder
898 W. 16th St.
Newport Beach, CA 92663

This is the magazine that first published the "Hey Kid!" series and that has always promoted all modeling as a matter of policy. Cost is $25 a year for monthly magazine.

Flying Models
PO BOx 700
Newton, NJ 07860

This is the magazine once known as *Flying Aces*. It has changed a lot since the 1930s, but it's still one of the better magazines. Monthly magazine is $23.00 per year.

BEGINNERS' MODEL BOOKS

Peck Polymers (see address on page 50)

Peck Polymers has several books in stock—including this one, one hopes! *Rubber-powered Model Airplanes* by Don Ross is one you might find useful.

Hannan's Runway
Box 210
Magaliz, CA 95954

Hannan's carries the Ross book; one on indoor scale models by Fred Hall; *Throw it Out of Sight* about hand-launched gliders; British model books with old-time models in them; and the Zaic Yearbooks, covering many types of historical and interesting models and subjects. Send $1.00 for the latest listings. In addition, Hannan's carries this book and the first one in the series.

Glossary

aileron a movable section of the rear of each wing which, when moved upward, forces the wing down, and vice versa.

building board a soft sheet of 1/2-inch-thick, fibrous material good for putting your plan over and sticking in the pins to hold parts down while building, painted white on one side and available at a lumber yard.

camber the curvature of the top of a wing to produce low pressure and lift.

cutting board a piece of cardboard, vinyl floor tile, or anything to keep from cutting up your mother's best table top or your model plan.

CyA "instant" or cyanoacrylate glue, not recommended for model use due to the hazard of possibly getting it into your eye.

dihedral the condition in which the wing tips are raised higher than the center where it attaches to the fuselage. This is an automatic righting feature which greatly helps the plane fly unaided.

dope a light plastic paint used to apply, seal, and strengthen fabric or tissue covering.

double-gluing putting a light coat of glue on a part, letting it soak in, and then applying the second coat before joining two parts.

doubler an extra thickness of wood glued over a break or a weak place in the model structure.

drag the force that tends to hold the model back as it flies either produced by making lift, air "rubbing" over the model, or just pushing the model through the air.

empennage the tail of the aircraft including the vertical and horizontal stabilizers and movable control surfaces.

epoxy an extremely strong glue which comes in two parts which need to be mixed before using. Keep away from eyes!

fuselage   the body of the model to which are attached the wing(s) and tail.

grain   the direction of the fibers in wood or tissue. Wood breaks and tissue tears easily along the grain direction.

"Green Tube" glue   refers to a cellulose acetate clear model glue for wood made by Testors, more correctly called "cement for wood models, fast drying, No. 3505." Good all-purpose cement.

gusset   a small triangle which is glued into a corner where two pieces of balsa meet to strengthen the corner.

LE   the front or "leading" edge of the wing.

lift   the force that makes the plane fly, generated by the camber and angle at which the wing and fuselage meet the relative wind.

longeron   one of the long sticks that form the corners of the fuselage "box," being the main structural members connecting the nose and tail.

music wire   a stiff, hardened steel wire coming in various sizes and often used for propeller shafts and landing gear legs. Sometimes called piano wire.

pitch   the angle at which the blades of a propeller (airscrew) are set to bite into the air and force it rearward to produce thrust. More angle or higher pitch gives less power but a longer run with a rubber motor. Low pitch runs out the winds in the motor faster, but gives more thrust.

pre-shrinking tissue   a process by which tissue paper used for model covering is sprayed with water mist while it is attached to a frame around the edges and allowed to tighten before it is attached to the model for warp prevention.

relative wind   the air the model is flying into, coming directly opposite the flight path.

rib   one of the parts that give the wing its airfoil shape, often cambered on top and flat on the bottom. The ribs connect the LE and the TE at intervals along the wing.

R.O.G.   Rise-Off-Ground. A model that begins flight touching the ground, usually on wheels.

rubber lube   a slippery substance applied to a rubber motor loop to allow it to accept more turns wound into it. Common rubber lubes contain glycerin and green soap, available at pharmacies and mixed together in about equal parts.

sanding block   a small, flat piece of wood to which is glued some fairly rough (80- to 100-grit) abrasive paper.

spar   one or more of the main structural members inside the wing which runs in the same direction as the LE and TE. The ribs attach to it.

stall   a condition in flight where the nose of the plane goes up so steeply that the model loses lift from the airflow breaking away from the top of the wing. Stalls are usually followed by the nose dropping until the air reattaches itself to the top of the wing, giving enough lift for another stall, followed by another drop, like a roller coaster.

TE   the rear or "trailing" edge of the wing.

thermal a rising mass of air warmed by the sun striking the ground. Models and birds can make use of these for long flights.

thrust the force which moves the model forward. Usually created by a propeller turned by an engine or twisted rubber strands.

torque reaction when the spinning propeller is going one way due to being twisted by the rubber motor, the rest of the model is being twisted in the opposite direction, causing the left wing to drop and the model to turn (and probably dive) to the left.

trimming out refers to making the model fly smoothly by adjusting the balance and/or the trim tabs.

trim tab a small control surface which is bendable to allow adjustments to be made in the flight of the model. These usually take the place of the pilot-operated ailerons, elevator, and rudder on a full-sized aircraft.

undercamber the inwardly-curved bottom surface of some wings which can force more air downward for more lift.

warp a twist in a flying surface (wing or stab usually) that can help or mess up a flight. Most warps are bad news and need to be steamed out over a tea kettle before you go flying.

wash-in a warp in a wing with the LE higher than the TE which tends to increase the lift on that wing and make it drag rearward a bit. Often used on the inside wing in a turn to compensate for the lift lost by that wing due to the bank produced by the turn, and by the inside wing moving slower than the outside wing.

wash-out the opposite of wash-in, with the TE higher than the LE. This is sometimes used on each wing tip to aid stability, especially on low-winged models because the wing tips are less efficient (usually smaller section) than wing roots and tend to stall sooner—a bad situation for stability.

winder a mechanical device used to wind up rubber motors, which are stretched to about double their length for winding. Commonly available winders have about a 5:1 ratio to 16:1, allowing the winds to be put in quickly. Sometimes hand drills are converted into winders by adding a hook anchored solidly in the chuck.

X-ing pins using two dressmaker's pins to hold a thin balsa stick down to the plan instead of sticking one through it and weakening it. They are leaned toward the stick from each side to provide location and downward pressure.

Index

A

A.A. Lidberg Plans, 49
air currents and winds, 22, 41
airfoils (*see* wings)
Allen Hunt Plan Service, 49
angle of attack, 16

B

balsa wood
    coloring or tinting, 36
    grain direction, 4, 6-7
    practicing printwood transfers, 4
banking, 23
bending jig, landing gear, 25-29
Blue Ridge Model Products, 50
brushes and tools, clean-up, 37
butyrate dope, 34

C

Champion Model Products, 50
clean-up, 37
climb, 40
coloring balsa wood, 36
connect-the-dots transfer method,
    printwood, 4-5
construction techniques, 11-23
    bending jig for landing gear, 25-29
    clean-up, 37
    covering wings, 31-33
    dope application, 34-37
    landing gear, 25-30
    nose construction, 16-17
    propeller shaft, 30-31
    spar notches, 11-12
    tail assembly, 16
    tail frame finishing, 17-21
    wing and pylon slider assembly,
        16
    wing construction, 13-16
    wing finishing, 17-21
covering wings, 31-33
cutting boards, 6

D

die-cut kits, 4
dihedral, 7-8, 15, 21-23
dihedral gauges, 8
dives, 40, 42-43
dope application, 34-37
    butyrate dope, 34
    nitrate dope, 34
    non-tautening dope, 34
    SIG Lite Coat dope, 34
    tautening dope, 34
downthrust, 20

E

Easy Built Models, 50
enlarging plans, 3
epoxy glue, 16

F

field selection for flying, 38-39
fillets, glue, 12
flying
    angle of attack, 16

climb, 40
downthrust, 20
dives, 40, 42-43
field selection, 38-39
left-hand turns only, 42
low-power test run, 12
pre-flight inspection, 37-38, 47
rubber winder, 37
stalls, 42-43
thermals, 41
trim tab adjustment, 39-40
troubleshooting chart, 42
vortex in air current, 41
"zoom" during high-power flight,
  20
Flying Models magazine, 51

G

gluing tips
  double gluing, 11-12
  epoxy glue, 16
  fillets, 12
  glue selection, 12
  "setting" the glue, 36-37
  Testors Green Tube glue, 12, 16
grain direction in balsa, 4, 6-7

H

Hannan's Runaway, 51

I

information sources, 51
iron-on transfer, printwood, 4-5

J

jeweler's rouge for knife sharpening,
  6

K

kits (*see* suppliers)
knife sharpening, 6

L

landing gear, 25-30
  bending jig construction, 25-29
  foot position, 27
  saddle or crossover, 27
  wheel attachment, 30
  wire bending techniques, 27-29
lateral stability, 8, 21-23
leading edge (LE), 4

M

magazines and newsletters, 51
Model Aviation magazine, 51

Model Builder magazine, 51

N

nitrate dope, 34
non-tautening dope, 34
nose construction, 16-17

P

Peck Polymers, 50, 51
plans, 44-46, 49-50
  A.A. Lidberg Plans, 49
  Allen Hunt Plan Service, 49
  copying and enlarging, 3
  make-your-own, 3
  studying plans before
    construction, 7-9
  transferring plans to printwood,
    4-5
pre-flight inspection, 37-38, 47
printwood construction, 4-5
  connect-the-dots transfer method,
    4-5
  iron-on transfer, 4-5
  solvent transfer, 4-5
propellers, 22
  shaft bending, 30-31
  shaft construction, 8
publications, 51
pylon assembly, 17
pylon slider assembly, 16

R

reinforcing wings, 33
root rib, 7, 15, 21
rubber winder, 37

S

sanding techniques, wing
    construction, 20-21
scratch-building
  clean-up, 37
  construction techniques, 11-23
  covering wings, 31-33
  cutting out parts, 4, 6
  dihedral, 7-8
  dope application, 34-37
  enlarging plans, 3
  grain direction in balsa, 4, 6-7
  landing gear, 25-30   materials and
    supplies, 1-3
  nose construction, 16-17
  plan-making, 3
  printwood construction, 4-5
  propeller shaft, 8
  root rib, 7

separating parts, 6-7
sharpening model knives, 6
spar notches, 11-12
studying plans before
  construction, 7-9
tail building, 16
thrust line, 8
wing and pylon slider assembly,
  16
sharpening model knives, 6
sideslipping, 23
SIG Lite Coat dope, 34
solvent transfer, printwood, 4-5
spar notches, lining-up, 11-12
stalls, 42-43
suppliers, 49-50
  A.A. Lidberg Plans, 49
  Allen Hunt Plan Service, 49
  Blue Ridge Model Products, 50
  Champion Model Products, 50
  Easy Built Models, 50
  Hannan's Runaway, 51
  Peck Polymers, 50, 51

T

tail construction, 16
  finishing touches, 17-21
tautening dope, 34
Testors Green Tube glue, 12, 16
thermals, 22, 41
thrust line, 8
tissue application, 31-33
torque reaction, 8
trailing edge (TE), 4
trim tab adjustment, 39-40

troubleshooting chart, 42
turns, 23, 42

V

vortex in air currents, 41

W

wheels (*see* landing gear)
whetstone for knife sharpening, 6
wind and air currents, 22, 41
wings
  construction techniques, 13-16
  covering, 31-33   dihedral
    measurement, 15, 21-23
  dope application, 34-37
  finishing touches, 17-21
  gluing halves together, 21
  leading edge (LE), 4, 20
  pylon assembly, 17
  pylon slider assembly, 16
  reinforcement piece, 33
  ribs, 14
  root rib, 7, 15, 21
  sanding techniques, 20-21
  "setting" the glue, 36-37
  trailing edge (LE), 4
  wobble-correction, 13
wire-bending techniques, 27-29
wobble correction, wing
  construction, 13

Z

"zoom" during high-power flight,
  downthrust, 20

Other Bestsellers of Related Interest

LEARN TO FLY RC HELICOPTERS
—Dale Hart

Here's your complete guide to RC helicopters—from choosing the right model to performing aerobatics. You'll learn to select your first kit and outfit it with the right engine, radio, control system, and other necessary components. Plus, you'll find clear, illustrated procedures for assembling, adjusting, and testing your models, as well as detailed advice on choosing a good flying site. 160 pages, 50 illustrations. **Book No. 3619, $12.95 paperback only**

THE SPORTFLIER'S GUIDE TO RC SOARING
—Jeff Troy

Here's a great way to get started in the hobby of building and flying radio-controlled (RC) airplanes. This clear, nontechnical introduction to the popular sport of RC soaring comes complete with flying techniques. Photographs and illustrations highlight building steps and the different types of equipment. Plus, photographs of completed models make it easy for you to select and reproduce the model of your choice. 176 pages, 177 illustrations. **Book No. 3519, $12.95 paperback only**

THE BEGINNER'S GUIDE TO FLYING ELECTRIC-POWERED AIRPLANES
—Douglas R. Pratt

Join the fastest-growing segment of the radio-control sport flying hobby—electric-powered airplanes! More and more flyers are discovering the advantages of clean, quiet electric power, and this book can help you make that discovery too. Pratt provides all the information you need on selecting, building, and flying these high-performance machines. He tells you what's needed in the way of motors, radios, control systems, chargers, and batteries, and how to get the most out of your model. 128 pages, 93 illustrations. **Book No. 3451, $12.95 paperback only**

THE BEGINNER'S GUIDE TO RADIO CONTROL SPORT FLYING
—Douglas R. Pratt

Building, flying, and repairing all different kinds of airplanes are covered in this guide. Safety guidelines are included and the author also discusses the Federal Communications Commission RC frequencies. This book contains enough technical information to keep your planes in the air and your equipment in good working condition. 160 pages, 80 illustrations. **Book No. 3020, $9.95 paperback only**

THE ADVANCED GUIDE TO RADIO CONTROL SPORT FLYING
—Douglas R. Pratt

This advanced volume provides greater detail in electrical and electronic aspects of the sport. The special considerations of choosing components for electric-powered flight are examined: cobalt or not cobalt; gear drives; battery selection; engine type; prop choice; motor control, and more. 160 pages, 86 illustrations. **Book No. 3060, $9.95 paperback only**

RC OVAL RACING
—Paul Crawford

Experience the excitement of Daytona for a lot less money than it takes to run the stocks. Convert your off-road 1/10-scale radio-controlled cars for oval track racing with this definitive, step-by-step guide. It covers every kit component modification, after-market product addition, set-up, and tuning techniques modelers need to transform their off-road racers into slick oval track winners. You get important in-depth coverage of winning techniques plus budget-minded options. 184 pages, 100 illustrations. **Book No. 3470, $12.95 paperback only**

BUILDING PLASTIC MODEL AIRCRAFT
—*Richard Marmo*

Discover the pleasure of constructing a fully detailed, authentic scale model of an aircraft or spacecraft with this beginner's guide to selecting, building, detailing, and displaying model airplanes. Dozens of practical tips, tricks, and techniques help you build better replicas—you'll even create a professional-quality model your first time! 96 pages, 4 color pages, 88 illustrations. **Book No. 2396, $9.95 paperback only**

ENCYCLOPAEDIA OF MILITARY MODELS 1/72 SCALE
—*Claude Boileau, Huynh-Dinh Khuong, and Thomas A. Young*

A complete guide to all 1/72 scale military models produced worldwide! Brief histories accompany full-color illustrations of kits and kitboxes manufactured at 1/72 scale throughout the world. Concise critiques evaluate the type and quality of kit materials and the accuracy of detail replicated in finished models. Model manufacturers (including addresses) comprise the entire second portion of the book. 204 pages, Illustrated in four-color. **Book No. 22383, $6.00 paperback, $9.00 hardcover**

MODEL CAR BUILDING: Advanced Techniques
—*Dennis Doty*

Advanced Techniques takes you beyond the basic construction of model cars to restyling, customizing, and designing techniques. Parts swapping, engine wiring, installing brake systems, top chopping both late-model and vintage model cars, and making many other modifications to kit building are among the advanced concepts explained in Doty's second volume. An in-depth look at the emergence of model car cottage industries examines the influence of this burgeoning sector. 128 pages, Over 150 illustrations. 4-page full-color section. **Book No. 3095, $10.95 paperback only**

THE HANDBOOK OF MODEL RAILROAD SCENERY AND DETAILING
—*Albert A. Sorensen*

Remarkably clear, step-by-step instructions and illustrations for the modeling, finishing, and detailing of all types of scale modeling scenery are outlined in this handbook. Following his own unique method, Albert Sorensen shows you how to add scenery and details to your layout by dividing the work into specific categories. 368 pages, 121 illustrations. 8 full-color pages. **Book No. 3420, $19.95 paperback only**

AMERICAN AVIATION: An Illustrated History
—*Joe Christy, with contributions by Alexander T. Wells, Ed.D.*

Here, in a comprehensive, well-researched sourcebook, Christy and Wells have taken the history of American aviation and transformed it into a fascinating story of people, machines, and accomplishments that is as entertaining as it is informative. With its hundreds of excellent photographs, this is a book that every aviation enthusiast will want to read and reread! 400 pages, 486 illustrations. **Book No. 2497, $25.95 paperback only**

THE FIRST TO FLY: Aviation's Pioneer Days
—*Sherwood Harris*

Based on diaries, letters, interviews, and newspaper reports, this book captures the color, adventure, resourcefulness, mechanical ingenuity, and perseverance of the men and women who turned their dreams of flying into reality. Whenever possible, the daring exploits of these fledgling aviators are told in their own words and the words of those who witnessed the great events that marked the early days of aviation, from 1900 to 1915. 240 pages, 72 illustrations. **Book No. 3796, $14.95 paperback, $24.95 hardcover**

STEALTH STRIKE
—Frank J. O'Brien

This suspense-packed novel is set in 1995. Star Wars satellites are up and the Russians want them down. The Soviets are so desperate to restore the status quo that they are willing to risk triggering World War III. The action builds and America's daring preemptive strike puts you in the cockpit, treating you to the longest, most grueling edge-of-the-seat dogfight you are ever likely to encounter. 276 pages. **Book No. 3472,** $16.95 hardcover only

SWEETWATER GUNSLINGER 201
—Lt. Commander William H. LaBarge, U.S. Navy and Robert Lawrence Holt

By the author of the current bestseller *Good Friday!* Set aboard the U.S. Carrier *Kitty Hawk* during the Iranian crisis of 1980, this fast-paced novel details the lives, loves, dangers, trials, tribulations, and escapades of a group of Tail Hookers (Navy carrier pilots). As much fact as fiction, it's a story that is both powerful and sensitive . . . by authors who do a masterful job of bringing the reader aboard a modern aircraft carrier and into the cockpit of an F-14! 192 pages. **Book No. 28515,** $14.95 hardcover only

THE LOG OF CHRISTOPHER COLUMBUS
—translated by Robert H. Fuson

"*I decided to write down everything that I might see and experience on this voyage, from day-to-day, and very carefully . . .*" So begins the most influential journal in nautical history. Robert H. Fuson, an eminent Columbus scholar, has painstakingly assembled the patchwork of notes and theories surrounding this historic voyage, resulting in an exciting tribute and moving story of this courageous accomplishment. Complete with handsome maps, photographs, woodcuts, and pen-and-ink illustrations. 272 pages, 15 illustrations. **Book No. 60660,** $14.95 paperback, $29.95 hardcover

Aero Series, Vol. 40, THE BOEING 747
—David H. Minton

Probably the single greatest contributor to worldwide flight, the Boeing 747 is in a class all its own. Now you can take part in each step of its evolution from its beginning as the world's first "wide body" jet to one of the most sophisticated, complex, and cost-efficient aircraft ever built. 128 pages, 61 illustrations. **Book No. 3574,** $10.95 paperback only

Look for These and Other TAB Books at Your Local Bookstore

To Order Call Toll Free 1-800-822-8158
(in PA, AK, and Canada call 717-794-2191)

or write to TAB Books, Blue Ridge Summit, PA 17294-0840.

Title	Product No.	Quantity	Price

☐ Check or money order made payable to TAB Books

Charge my ☐ VISA ☐ MasterCard ☐ American Express

Acct. No. _____ Exp. _____

Signature: _____

Name: _____

Address: _____

City: _____

State: _____ Zip: _____

Subtotal $ _____

Postage and Handling
($3.00 in U.S., $5.00 outside U.S.) $ _____

Add applicable state and local
sales tax $ _____

TOTAL $ _____

TAB Books catalog free with purchase; otherwise send $1.00 in check or money order and receive $1.00 credit on your next purchase.

Orders outside U.S. must pay with international money order in U.S. dollars.

TAB Guarantee: If for any reason you are not satisfied with the book(s) you order, simply return it (them) within 15 days and receive a full refund.
BC